Positive Affect Treatment for Depression and Anxiety

 **TREATMENTS** THAT WORK

Positive Affect Treatment for Depression and Anxiety

THERAPIST GUIDE

MICHELLE G. CRASKE

HALINA J. DOUR

MICHAEL TREANOR

ALICIA E. MEURET

OXFORD
UNIVERSITY PRESS

OXFORD
UNIVERSITY PRESS

Oxford University Press is a department of the University of Oxford. It furthers the University's objective of excellence in research, scholarship, and education by publishing worldwide. Oxford is a registered trade mark of Oxford University Press in the UK and certain other countries.

Published in the United States of America by Oxford University Press
198 Madison Avenue, New York, NY 10016, United States of America.

Library of Congress Cataloging-in-Publication Data
Names: Craske, Michelle G., 1959- editor. | Dour, Halina J., editor. |
Treanor, Michael, editor.
Title: Positive affect treatment for depression and anxiety : therapist guide /
edited by Michelle G. Craske, Halina J. Dour, Michael Treanor, and Alicia E. Meuret.
Description: New York, NY : Oxford University Press, [2022] |
Includes bibliographical references and index.
Identifiers: LCCN 2022003281 (print) | LCCN 2022003282 (ebook) |
ISBN 9780197548523 (paperback) | ISBN 9780197548530 (epub) |
ISBN 9780197548554
Subjects: LCSH: Depression in adolescence—Treatment. |
Depression in children—Treatment. | Anxiety in adolescence—Treatment. |
Anxiety in children—Treatment.
Classification: LCC RJ506.D4 P67 2022 (print) | LCC RJ506.D4 (ebook) |
DDC 616.85/2700835—dc23/eng/20220217
LC record available at https://lccn.loc.gov/2022003281
LC ebook record available at https://lccn.loc.gov/2022003282

DOI: 10.1093/med-psych/9780197548523.001.0001

9 8 7 6 5 4 3 2 1

Printed by Marquis, Canada

About ✓TREATMENTS THAT WORK

Stunning developments in healthcare have taken place over the last several years, but many of our widely accepted interventions and strategies in mental health and behavioral medicine have been brought into question by research evidence as not only lacking benefit, but perhaps, inducing harm (Barlow, 2010). Other strategies have been proven effective using the best current standards of evidence, resulting in broad-based recommendations to make these practices more available to the public (McHugh & Barlow, 2010). Several recent developments are behind this revolution. First, we have arrived at a much deeper understanding of pathology, both psychological and physical, which has led to the development of new, more precisely targeted interventions. Second, our research methodologies have improved substantially, such that we have reduced threats to internal and external validity, making the outcomes more directly applicable to clinical situations. Third, governments around the world and healthcare systems and policymakers have decided that the quality of care should improve, that it should be evidence based, and that it is in the public's interest to ensure that this happens (Barlow, 2004; Institute of Medicine, 2001, 2015; McHugh & Barlow, 2010).

Of course, the major stumbling block for clinicians everywhere is the accessibility of newly developed evidence-based psychological interventions. Workshops and books can go only so far in acquainting responsible and conscientious practitioners with the latest behavioral health care practices and their applicability to individual patients. This series, Treatments *That Work*™, is devoted to communicating these exciting new interventions to clinicians on the frontlines of practice.

The manuals and workbooks in this series contain step-by-step detailed procedures for assessing and treating specific problems and diagnoses. But this series also goes beyond the books and manuals by providing ancillary materials that will approximate the supervisory process in assisting practitioners in the implementation of these procedures in their practice.

In our emerging healthcare system, the growing consensus is that evidence-based practice offers the most responsible course of action for the mental health professional. All behavioral health care clinicians deeply desire to provide the best possible care for their patients. In this series, our aim is to close the dissemination and information gap and make that possible.

A substantial number of individuals with depression or anxiety experience anhedonia, or loss of interest or joy in usual activities. Anhedonia is a risk factor for poor prognosis and suicidality, and yet treatments to date have been relatively ineffective for anhedonia. Based on advances in behavioral and neuroscience, Positive Affect Treatment (PAT) was developed to specifically target areas of reward sensitivity that are believed to contribute to anhedonia. These include the anticipation and motivation for reward, the response to attainment of reward, and the learning of associations between actions and reward outcomes.

The guide is intended to be used by clinicians who are familiar with cognitive–behavioral therapy (CBT) generally and with clinical presentation of depression, anxiety, and anhedonia. Results show that PAT not only improves positive mood state but also decreases depression and anxiety. This therapist guide will be an indispensable resource for all practitioners who wish to effectively and efficiently help individuals regain interest and enjoyment in their usual activities while improving their quality of life.

David H. Barlow, Editor-in-Chief
Treatments *That Work*™
Boston, Massachusetts

References

Barlow, D. H. (2004). Psychological treatments. *American Psychologist, 59*, 869–878.

Barlow, D. H. (2010). Negative effects from psychological treatments: A perspective. *American Psychologist, 65*(2), 13–20.

Institute of Medicine. (2001). *Crossing the quality chasm: A new health system for the 21st century.* National Academy Press.

Institute of Medicine. (2015). *Psychosocial interventions for mental and substance use disorders: A framework for establishing evidence-based standards.* National Academies Press.

McHugh, R. K., & Barlow, D. H. (2010). Dissemination and implementation of evidence-based psychological interventions: A review of current efforts. *American Psychologist, 65*(2), 73–84.

Contents

Psychoeducation

CHAPTER 1 — Introductory Information for Therapists

(Corresponds to chapter 1 of the workbook)

Background Information and Purpose of This Program

Anhedonia is a symptom cluster involving loss of interest or joy in usual activities. Typical client statements that are indicative of anhedonia include "I just don't find anything to be enjoyable," "Things that I used to enjoy seem like a chore," or "What is the point of trying? I never feel good." Anhedonia is a transdiagnostic symptom that characterizes many individuals suffering from depression, as well as some types of anxiety, psychosis, and substance use. To date, anhedonia has been relatively unresponsive to psychological and pharmacological treatments. Yet, anhedonia is a significant marker of a poor long-term course for depression, as well as a poor response to existing treatments, both psychological and pharmacological. Furthermore, anhedonia is a robust predictor of suicidality, including suicide attempts, above and beyond other symptoms. Thus, anhedonia represents a significant marker of psychopathology and of risk.

Part of the reason why existing psychological and pharmacological treatments have had limited effect on anhedonia is their lack of focus on its underlying mechanisms. Advances in behavioral science and neuroscience, including work from our own laboratories, have found specific mechanisms that may contribute to anhedonia. These mechanisms converge on deficits in reward responsiveness—specifically, deficits in the anticipation of reward or motivation to work for reward, deficits in the savoring or appreciation of reward, and deficits in the learning of reward. The majority of treatments to date have focused almost exclusively on decreasing the negative valence associated with the defensive system rather than addressing deficits in the reward system (Craske et al., 2016). We saw a need for a new treatment approach that specifically targets deficits in the reward system, which we call Positive Affect Treatment (PAT; Craske et al., 2019). This therapist guide, which accompanies the PAT workbook for clients, describes the underlying principles and procedures of PAT.

What Is Anhedonia?

Lack of enjoyment in and lack of desire for usual activities are the core features of anhedonia (American Psychiatric Association, 2016). Low levels of positive emotions are key to anhedonia. A substantial number of individuals with depression are estimated to have clinically significant anhedonia as defined by cutoffs on scales that measure enjoyment of social and physical pleasure (Pelizza & Ferrari, 2009). However, anhedonia is not limited to depression. A body of evidence contradicts earlier models that linked positive affect almost exclusively to depression relative to anxiety (Brown et al., 1998; Clark & Watson, 1991). In fact, effect sizes for cross-sectional and longitudinal relationships between positive affect and anxiety are significant and indistinguishable from corresponding effect sizes for positive affect and depression (Khazanov & Ruscio, 2016; Kotov et al., 2010). Moreover, hedonic impairments have been observed in social anxiety disorder (Kashdan et al., 2011), posttraumatic stress disorder (Hopper et al., 2008; Litz et al., 2000), and generalized anxiety disorder (Srivastava et al., 2003), including youth samples (Morris et al., 2015).

Anhedonia is a major marker of psychopathology. For example, anhedonia prospectively predicts both depression and anxiety, even when controlling for baseline symptoms (Kendall et al., 2015; Khazanov & Ruscio, 2016). Once disorders emerge, anhedonia is a robust predictor of a poorer longitudinal course of major depression (Morris et al., 2009). Further, anhedonia predicts poor psychosocial functioning after improvements in depressed mood (Vinckier et al., 2017) and recurrence of depression (Wichers et al., 2010). Moreover, anhedonia is a substantial predictor of suicidal ideation and attempt (Ducasse et al., 2018; Spijker et al., 2010; Winer et al., 2014). In over 2500 clients with mood disorders, those with anhedonia had a 1.4-fold higher risk of suicidal ideation in the next three years (Ducasse et al., 2021). The predictive effects on suicidal ideation or attempt persist when controlling for other cognitive and affective symptoms of depression (Ballard et al., 2017; Fawcett et al., 1990), as well as other risk factors such as history of suicide attempts, childhood trauma, marital status, sex, and age (Ducasse et al., 2021). Finally, anhedonia statistically accounts for the relation between depression and suicidality (Zielinski et al., 2017).

Existing Treatments Are Inadequate for Anhedonia

Clients with depression often view the restoration of positive mood as their primary treatment goal, over reducing negative symptoms (Demyttenaere et al., 2015). Yet, extant treatments are inadequate to address positive mood. Specifically, standard medication treatments have mixed effects and may even worsen positive emotions or responses to rewarding stimuli (Landén et al., 2005; McCabe et al., 2010; Nierenberg et al., 1999; Price et al., 2009), although newer pharmacological approaches such as kappa-opioid antagonism and ketamine are showing promising effects (Ballard et al., 2017; Pizzagalli et al., 2020; Thomas et al., 2018). Evidence-based psychotherapies (primarily cognitive–behavioral therapy [CBT] and mindfulness-based cognitive therapy) have limited effects on positive affect (Boumparis et al., 2016). For example, in a reanalysis of DeRubeis et al. (2005), cognitive therapy and antidepressant medication normalized elevations in negative affect but had little effect on positive affect measured using the Positive and Negative Affect Schedule (PANAS) (Watson et al., 1988). Even behavioral activation therapy, which aims to increase positive affect through response-contingent positive reinforcement from rewarding activities (Martell et al., 2010), has limited effects on positive affect or anhedonia in the few studies in which such effects have been reported (Dichter et al., 2009; Moore et al., 2013). This is perhaps not surprising since little attention has been given to how to conduct behavioral activation in a manner that maximizes rewarding, positive emotional experiences (Dunn, 2012; Forbes, 2020). We proposed that treatment effects will be bolstered by targeting processes thought to underlie anhedonia, including deficits in reward responsiveness. Our Positive Affect Treatment (Craske et al., 2016, 2019) is designed specifically to target deficits in reward responsiveness for symptoms of anhedonia.

Efficacy of PAT

In our randomized controlled trial for clients with clinically significant and impairing anxiety or depression, we compared PAT to a cognitive-behaviorally based intervention called Negative Affect Treatment [NAT]. NAT included exposure to distressing and avoided situations, cognitive restructuring to reduce overestimates of threat, catastrophizing and attributions of self-blame, and arousal regulation through respiratory training. PAT included behavioral activation to rewarding experiences augmented by savoring the moment; cognitive tools for increasing attention to positive stimuli; and cultivation of positive emotions through mood-boosting exercises of appreciative joy, gratitude, generosity, and loving-kindness. The treatment was implemented over 15 individual sessions. Clients were randomized to either treatment condition, and assessments were completed at baseline, throughout treatment, at posttreatment, and at six months follow-up.

PAT resulted in greater improvements in positive affect than NAT (Craske et al., 2019). Figure 1.1A represents the change in positive affect, measured using the Positive Affect Scale of the PANAS, for PAT and NAT. Clients had very low positive affect at treatment outset (below the 15th percentile of population norms), but values for those in the PAT group reached the population norm at the end of treatment and following treatment. This is the first demonstration of a psychological

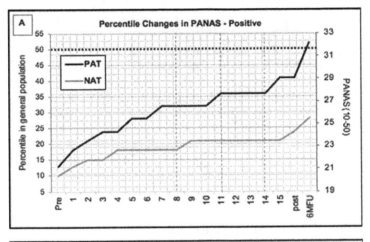

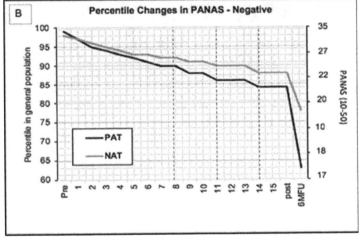

Figure 1.1

Changes in positive affect (A) and negative affect (B), measured using the PANAS, in Positive Affect Treatment (PAT) and Negative Affect Treatment (NAT).

treatment that normalizes positive affect in clients with depression or anxiety. Figure 1.1B also shows that PAT was more effective than NAT in reducing negative affect.

Participants in PAT also reported superior reductions in depression, anxiety, stress, and suicidality at the six-month follow-up. As shown in Figure 1.2, depression, anxiety, and stress were very high at baseline and decreased into a normal (non-clinical) range over the course

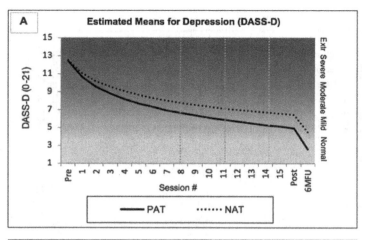

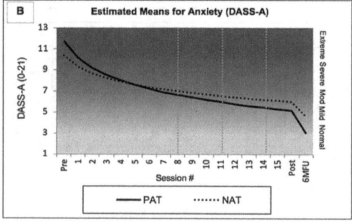

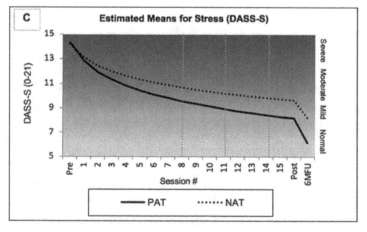

Figure 1.2

Changes in depression (A), anxiety (B), and stress (C), measured using the Depression, Anxiety, and Stress Scale, in PAT and NAT.

of treatment and follow-up (six months after treatment). We have replicated these initial effects in a second randomized controlled trial (publication forthcoming).

Who Will Benefit from PAT?

As noted, PAT was developed specifically to address deficits or dysregulation in reward responsiveness that characterize anhedonia, or the loss of interest or joy in usual activities. Our PAT trial was conducted with individuals who presented with levels of depression and anxiety and anhedonia that were above clinical severity cutoffs, and the majority were diagnosed with either an anxiety disorder or a major depressive disorder, or both. Nonetheless, we would also expect the program to be useful in treating symptoms of depression and anxiety in clients who do not meet the full diagnostic clinical criteria, as well as individuals who score subthreshold on severity criteria, but are at risk for full disorder status.

Aside from depression and anxiety, anhedonia is characteristic of individuals with substance use, trauma, eating disorders, and schizophrenia. To date, PAT has been evaluated only in individuals who present with depression or anxiety and has not been tested in individuals with other disorders. Nonetheless, we expect that it will be helpful when tailored to the needs of individuals with other disorders as well.

During the initial client assessment, it can be helpful to complete Exercise 2.1: Treatment Fit Assessment and Exercise 2.2: Treatment Timing Assessment, which can be found in chapter 2 of the client workbook (on page 16 and 17) and also in the appendix at the end of this therapist guide. You may photocopy these assessments or download multiple copies at the Treatments *That Work*™ website (www.oxfordclinicalpsych.com/PAT).

What If Other Emotional Problems Are Present?

The evidence strongly suggests high levels of overlap across the various anxiety disorders and mood disorders both at the diagnostic level and the symptomatic level. This is why current and lifetime diagnostic comorbidity are observed across the anxiety and mood disorders (e.g., Kessler et al., 2005). It is very common for individuals with one anxiety disorder to have another anxiety disorder or a mood disorder, and similarly for individuals with a principal mood disorder to also have an anxiety disorder. The presence of multiple disorders, however, does not preclude the use of PAT. In fact, PAT was developed specifically to target the underlying dimension of anhedonia that cuts across distinct diagnostic entities of specific anxiety disorders and mood disorders. Notably, the majority of study participants suffered from comorbid anxiety and mood disorders.

Role of Medication

Clients often seek psychological treatment for emotional problems, including anhedonia, while already taking psychotropic medications. Some clients present to our clinics having been prescribed low doses of high-potency benzodiazepines such as alprazolam (Xanax) or clonazepam (Klonopin), or antidepressants including selective serotonin reuptake inhibitors (SSRIs) such as paroxetine (Paxil) or fluoxetine (Prozac), serotonin–norepinephrine reuptake inhibitors (SNRIs) such as venlafaxine (Effexor), or tricyclic antidepressants such as clomipramine. The effects of combining medications with PAT are not yet understood and await further investigation. Thus, we do not recommend that clients discontinue medications before initiating PAT, rather they should continue on a stable medication dose. Unless clinically necessary, we usually discourage clients from increasing dosages of medication or beginning new medications during treatment. This is because medication changes can interfere with therapeutic strategies and with evaluation of the medication's effectiveness. This can become confusing for the therapist and frustrating for the client and may ultimately lead to poorer treatment outcomes.

Certain psychotropic medications have anhedonic side effects (Landén et al., 2005; McCabe et al., 2010; Price et al., 2009). Thus, it might be advisable for clients who are currently taking psychotropic medications to discuss with their prescriber the possibility that their anhedonic symptoms are related to medications.

Who Should Administer the Program?

The treatment concepts and techniques are presented in detail in the corresponding client workbook so that the mental health professional can supervise its implementation. Nonetheless, we do recommend that therapists are familiar with basic principles of cognitive–behavioral interventions. The therapist should also have a good understanding of the principles underlying the treatment procedures in the client workbook. This will allow the therapist to adapt the material to suit the needs of each client and to overcome difficulties and barriers in the treatment should they arise. We also recommend that the therapist become familiar with the nature of anhedonia using some of the basic information presented in this therapist guide along with the recommended readings that we provide.

Benefits of Using the Client Workbook

While it may appear that clients have a good understanding of the material that is presented by the therapist during session, it is not uncommon for them to misremember or forget important points. One of the greatest benefits of a client workbook is that it provides a review of treatment concepts, explanations, and instructions that the client can read between sessions. It also is an immediate reference that clients can use to help guide themselves when they experience anhedonic symptoms. This can be important because they can apply the learning process as the need is emerging, which may in turn lead to greater understanding of the treatment concepts and better appreciation of how to apply these procedures effectively.

Having the client workbook available allows clients to move at their own pace. Some may wish to move more quickly through the program by scheduling more frequent sessions, while others may choose to move more slowly due to conflicting demands such as work or travel. Having the client workbook available between scheduled sessions for review or rereading can be quite beneficial. Having the workbook also ensures that clients have a ready resource to refer back to after treatment ends. Clients will likely experience times when they need to revisit treatment content. The workbook is an essential resource to remind clients of what they learned and what they can continue to practice. Further, if the workbook is insufficient, they can request booster sessions with their therapist.

CHAPTER 2

Behavioral Science and Neuroscience Identify Targets for Treatment of Anhedonia

(Corresponds to chapters 1 and 2 of client workbook)

Targets for Treating Anhedonia: Reward Processes

It has long been recognized that at least two core systems regulate thoughts and behaviors or actions. An *approach* or *appetitive system* that motivates actions toward goals and rewards is linked with positive emotions such as enthusiasm and pride. A *withdrawal* or *defensive system* that motivates avoidance of aversive outcomes or punishments is linked with negative emotions such as fear and sadness (Lang & Bradley, 2013; Lang & Davis, 2006; Shankman & Klein, 2003). Our decision-making and survival depend on striking a balance between the defensive system to protect ourselves from dangers and the appetitive system to achieve the nutrients and nurturing to survive. Should we enter an unfamiliar and thereby potentially risky situation or avoid it at the cost of losing a potential social or monetary reward? We need the defensive system to remain safe and the appetitive system to accomplish our goals and feel satisfied and happy.

Anxiety and depression have long been understood to involve excesses in the defensive system, or an elevated threat responsivity. This would explain features such as increased hypothalamic–pituitary–adrenal (HPA) axis and physiological stress responses, increased bias to attend to threat and to interpret ambiguous situations as threatening, and increased tendencies to avoid potentially threatening situations. More recently, the role of deficits in the appetitive reward system, or lowered reward sensitivity, has been recognized. These deficits explain features such as lowered physiological arousal to and self-reported interest in the anticipation of reward or the receipt of reward, lowered sustained attention to positive stimuli, and lowered effort to gain reward.

While researchers emphasize different parts of the reward system, there is some convergence upon three main components (Figure 2.1; Der-Avakian & Markou, 2012; Thomsen et al., 2015):

- *Anticipation or motivation for reward* (wanting) is interest in future rewarding experiences and the effort expended to receive reward.
- *Responsivity to attainment of reward* (liking) refers to the pleasure or hedonic impact of reward, noticing when something rewarding happens and appreciating it.

Deficits In	Reward System	
- Getting motivated to do positive activities - Putting effort into positive activities - Imagining positive outcomes - Being interested in the positive	- Reward motivation - Reward anticipation	**Wanting**
- Noticing the positive - Appreciating the positive - Feeling positive emotions	- Reward attainment	**Liking**
- Learning what leads to rewards - Learning how to obtain rewards	- Reward learning	**Learning**

Figure 2.1

Parts of the reward system and associated deficits of anhedonia.

Clipart sourced from Microsoft PowerPoint.

- *Learning of reward* (learning) involves Pavlovian or instrumental associations and predictions about future rewards based on past experiences (i.e., learning what actions lead to rewards and what stimuli are rewarding).

In the client workbook, these three components are shown in Figure 1.1 in chapter 1.

The brain's reward circuitry encompasses regions of the basal ganglia, notably the ventral and dorsal striatum and the prefrontal cortex, particularly the orbitofrontal cortex (Berridge & Kringelbach, 2015; Mahler et al., 2007; Peters & Büchel, 2010). Functional neuroimaging studies report consistent activation of this circuitry during the initial response, anticipation of reward, and learning of reward. There is compelling evidence for strong links between low positive mood and reward hyposensitivity across the three components (McFarland & Klein, 2009; Pizzagalli et al., 2008; Thomsen et al., 2015).

Specifically, anhedonic symptoms of loss of pleasure or interest are associated with deficits in ventral striatum responsivity to anticipation of reward (Greenberg et al., 2015; Stoy et al., 2012; Ubl et al., 2015). At the behavioral level, the effort expended to obtain rewards correlates negatively with anhedonia (Treadway et al., 2012; Yang et al., 2014). Together, evidence suggests that anhedonia is associated with neural and behavioral deficits in the anticipation and motivation of reward, or deficits in wanting of reward.

In terms of reward attainment, ventral striatum hypoactivity to positive stimuli is particularly related to anhedonic symptoms relative to depression symptoms more broadly (Chung & Barch, 2015; Pizzagalli et al., 2009; Wacker et al., 2009). Similarly, reports of weaker positive emotions to positive stimuli are more strongly related to symptoms of anhedonia than symptoms of depression after excluding anhedonia (Clepce et al., 2010). Furthermore, anhedonia is associated with reduced cardiac acceleration while viewing pleasant pictorial stimuli or imagining pleasant emotional scripts (Fiorito & Simons, 1994; Fitzgibbons & Simons, 1992). Together, evidence suggests that anhedonia is associated with deficits in neural, subjective, and physiological responses when reward is attained, or deficits in liking of reward.

For reward learning, blunted ventral striatal responses to instrumental conditioning tasks correlate with anhedonic symptoms (Gradin et al.,

2011; Whitton et al., 2015). Also, impairments in a response bias to stimuli that are frequently rewarded correlate with anhedonia and predict anhedonic symptoms in the future (Pizzagalli et al., 2005, 2008; Vrieze et al., 2013). Overall, the evidence suggests that anhedonia is associated with deficits in neural and behavioral indicators of learning what is rewarding or how to obtain rewarding outcomes.

In the Positive Affect Treatment (PAT) client workbook, we state:

> For example, it can be hard for someone with anhedonia to look forward to positive events, feel good when there is a positive event, and know how to make themselves feel more positive. It is as if the mood system that regulates positive emotions is not working so well.

For these reasons, PAT was designed to specifically target the anticipation and motivation for reward, the initial response to reward attainment, and the learning of reward. Every aspect of the PAT program is designed to improve reward responsiveness. As you will see, clients often feel drawn to focus on the negative parts of their experience, to dwell on the worst, and to analyze the most negative parts of their lives to try to understand their reasons, or to fix them. In contrast, PAT takes the approach of focusing on building capacity to look forward to, attend to, enjoy and savor, and learn about positive and rewarding experiences. The premise is that by building capacity for reward, not only will rewarding experiences be felt more strongly (rather than being dismissed) but negative experiences (internal or external) will also become less predominant. We further present to clients that building the capacity for positivity will enable them to be better able to manage the negative experiences of life.

Skills to Build Wanting, Liking, and Learning Reward

In the psychoeducation module, we begin by providing the science and theory behind each PAT skill. Guided by behavioral science and affective neuroscience, we developed PAT to specifically address the major components of reward responsiveness that have shown to be dysregulated as a function of anhedonia (Craske et al., 2016). The components of PAT and their primary reward system targets are shown in Figure 2.2, which includes the corresponding chapters in the client workbook.

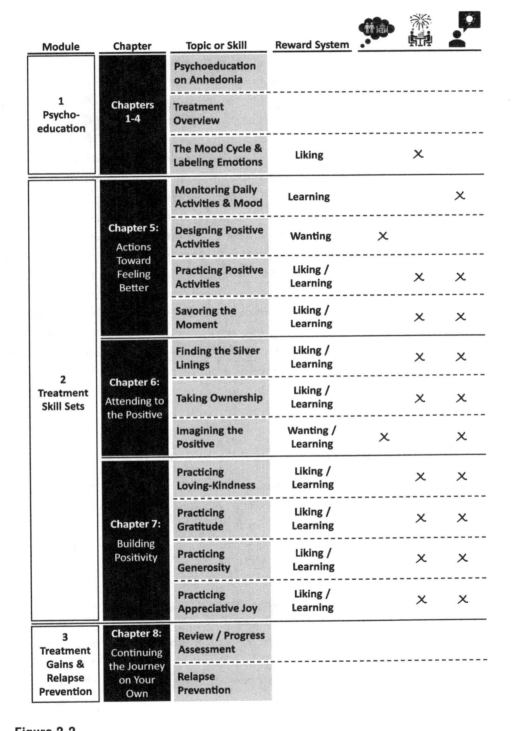

Module	Chapter	Topic or Skill	Reward System			
1 Psycho-education	**Chapters 1-4**	**Psychoeducation on Anhedonia**				
		Treatment Overview				
		The Mood Cycle & Labeling Emotions	Liking		✗	
2 Treatment Skill Sets	**Chapter 5:** Actions Toward Feeling Better	**Monitoring Daily Activities & Mood**	Learning			✗
		Designing Positive Activities	Wanting	✗		
		Practicing Positive Activities	Liking / Learning		✗	✗
		Savoring the Moment	Liking / Learning		✗	✗
	Chapter 6: Attending to the Positive	**Finding the Silver Linings**	Liking / Learning		✗	✗
		Taking Ownership	Liking / Learning		✗	✗
		Imagining the Positive	Wanting / Learning	✗		✗
	Chapter 7: Building Positivity	**Practicing Loving-Kindness**	Liking / Learning		✗	✗
		Practicing Gratitude	Liking / Learning		✗	✗
		Practicing Generosity	Liking / Learning		✗	✗
		Practicing Appreciative Joy	Liking / Learning		✗	✗
3 Treatment Gains & Relapse Prevention	**Chapter 8:** Continuing the Journey on Your Own	**Review / Progress Assessment**				
		Relapse Prevention				

Figure 2.2

Overview of skills in the modules and chapters.

Clipart sourced from Microsoft PowerPoint.

Labeling Emotions

Following psychoeducation and the description of cognitive, behavioral, and physiological components of mood cycles, Module 1 teaches the skill of emotion labeling for positive emotions. Individuals who are depressed can have difficulties identifying or labeling their emotions (alexithymia) (Honkalampi et al., 2001). Since individuals with anhedonia experience fewer positive emotional states overall, their repertoire for describing positive emotions is typically limited. Building this repertoire requires discriminating among different intensities and types of positive emotions (e.g., joy, thrill, contentment), and such discrimination facilitates attention to and encoding of internal states (e.g., feelings or thoughts) associated with each positive emotion. Training clients to attend to internal states associated with hedonic feelings offsets the deficits in sustained attention to positive stimuli that characterizes depression and anhedonia (Shane & Peterson, 2007), with a preference to attend to negative stimuli (Koster et al., 2005). Hence, the process of labeling positive emotions is likely to enhance attention to positive experiences, which will increase the attainment of reward.

Actions Toward Feeling Better

Following psychoeducation about the mood cycle and labeling of emotions, Module 2 presents the three treatment skill sets in PAT. Chapter 5 instructs clients how to plan and practice positive activities by *Savoring the Moment* through memory specificity training, to enhance hedonic impact. The first part draws heavily from original models of behavioral activation therapy that was designed to increase engagement in rewarding experiences (Lewinsohn & Libet, 1972). Behavioral activation involves designing and practicing daily activities that are inherently pleasurable, those that provide a sense of accomplishment or mastery, or those that are consistent with valued actions. The *Designing Positive Activities* skill targets the anticipation and motivation for reward, or wanting, and the *Practicing Positive Activities* skill targets response to attainment of reward, or liking. Detailed labeling of the positive emotions experienced during the activities facilitates the attainment or appreciation of reward, or liking. Changes in mood are closely monitored from before to after each activity to reinforce the positive mood-inducing effects; doing so targets reward learning (i.e., instrumental learning by which engaging in a specific activity increases positive mood or overall mood).

Equally important, if not more so, is the subsequent memory specificity training to target the attainment or savoring of reward (we call it *Savoring the Moment*). *Savoring the Moment* represents a departure from behavioral activation therapy. Such memory enhancement is essential because of a number of features that are characteristic of depression and that impede the savoring and learning of reward. These features are:

- Impoverished positive mental imagery. Individuals with depression have more negative mental imagery and deficits in generating vivid past-oriented (Werner-Seidler & Moulds, 2011) or future-oriented (Stöber, 2000) positive mental images and prospections (Yang et al., 2018) than do individuals without depression.
- Bias for a third-person perspective (vs. a first-person one), which leads to less positive emotionality (Holmes et al., 2008a; Mcisaac & Eich, 2002).
- Overly general autobiographical memory (Holmes et al., 2016), or failure to generate specific memories that take place within the span of a single event or single day (Williams et al., 2007), which is a predictor of the onset of depression and poorer course of depression (Barry et al., 2019; Brewin, 2006).
- A deficiency in positive self-representations (Brewin, 2006).

For these reasons, individuals with depression undervalue positive memories, as shown by decreased willingness to spend money for the opportunity to recall positive memories (Speer et al., 2014). Devaluation of positive memories likely contributes to ineffectiveness of standard behavioral activation therapy in terms of anhedonia outcomes, since the standard approach involves only guidance to engage in pleasurable activities and does not address memories for such activities. To target these abnormalities, our memory specificity training (for *Savoring the Moment*) involves visualizing assigned activities, including specific sensations, thoughts, emotions, and situational details, through first-person perspective and present tense. Our approach resembles other memory specificity interventions for emotional disorders that have led to short-term significant improvements in overly negative general memory, depression, hopelessness, problem-solving, anticipatory pleasure, and behavioral intention to engage in activities (Barry et al., 2019; Hallford et al., 2020a, 2020b; McMakin et al., 2011; Pictet et al., 2016). However, in PAT, the primary goal of *Savoring the Moment* is to enhance the hedonic impact of reward and to improve the skill of appreciating and liking a rewarding event.

During memory specificity training for *Savoring the Moment*, participants are guided to close their eyes, visualize, and recount in present tense the moment-to-moment details (surroundings, emotions, physical sensation, and thoughts), while focusing on the most positive experiences within the experienced activity. Through being repeatedly guided to attend to their physical sensations, thoughts, behaviors, and positive mood, the recounting is designed to deepen and savor the positive aspects of the experience. Other processes are likely taking place through *Savoring the Moment*. For example, the guided memory recounting involves shifting attention away from negative portions and toward positive portions of the behavioral experience. This is serving as a type of attentional control (shifting attention from one aspect of a situation to another). Such attentional control has been shown to be effective as a form of emotion regulation (Gross, 1998).

Additionally, memory specificity training involves sustained attention to positive stimuli, which itself has been shown to lead to subsequent preferences for positive stimuli, albeit in nonclinical samples (Wadlinger & Isaacowitz, 2008). Increased preference for positive material is posited to in turn decrease interest in negative information (Wadlinger & Isaacowitz, 2011). Furthermore, training positive attentional preferences may enhance attentional vigilance for and orienting toward positive information that eventually shifts more elaborate attention mechanisms in the direction of positive meanings. This facilitates encoding of positive information in daily experiences. Consequently, training attention to positive features of experience is likely to increase positive affect, perhaps via attentional processes that reinforce positive affect, and is posited to increase tendencies to approach rewards in the environment (Wadlinger & Isaacowitz, 2011).

Attending to the Positive

Chapter 6 comprises a set of cognitive training skills for attending to positive stimuli. Unlike cognitive therapy for depression, which challenges negative cognitions, PAT cognitive techniques aim to identify and savor positive aspects of experience (liking), take responsibility for positive outcomes (liking and learning), and imagine and appreciate future positive events (wanting). Hence, the PAT cognitive skill set does not address negative thoughts, or errors in thinking that may have contributed to negative assumptions and beliefs. Instead, the discussion is focused on attending to positive features of experiences in the past, present, and future. The cognitive skills primarily involve attention training without direct attempts to develop alternative appraisals. Targeting attention is expected to impact mood for the same reasons specified earlier (i.e., increases in positive affect, increases in preference for positive stimuli, decreased interest in negative stimuli, and eventual shift toward more positive meanings). Hence, even though there is little direct attempt to change negative appraisals, underlying meanings and appraisals may shift in a more positive direction. One exception is the skill of *Taking Ownership* where clients are asked to consider ways in which they may have contributed to a positive outcome, which in turn is likely to more directly influence self-appraisals.

The first cognitive training skill, *Finding the Silver Linings*, trains clients to recognize and appreciate the positive features in everyday situations, even situations that are negative. The repeated practice of identifying multiple positive elements in everyday situations is presumed to enhance preference for, attentional vigilance to, and encoding of positive information (Wadlinger & Isaacowitz, 2011).

The second skill, *Taking Ownership*, involves repeated practice of identifying one's own behavioral contributions to positive outcomes in daily lives (learning) and to savor positive emotions of pride, mastery, and excitement (wanting). Accomplishments can be read out loud in front of a mirror to deepen the experience of receipt of reward. *Taking Ownership* counters the depressive attributional bias to attribute positive outcomes to external factors and is consistent with experimental evidence for training toward a positive attributional bias (Peters et al., 2011).

The third skill, *Imagining the Positive*, is based on evidence in favor of enhanced positive mood and improvements in interpretation bias effects following repeated practice of imagining positive events (Holmes et al., 2006, 2008b; Pictet et al., 2011). *Imagining the Positive* was drawn from experimental protocols by Holmes and colleagues in which participants repeatedly imagine positive outcomes to ambiguous scenarios, as well as the work of others showing the deficits in generation of positive images for the future as a function of depressed mood (MacLeod et al., 1993). In PAT, clients are guided to repeatedly imagine as many positive aspects as possible about an upcoming event, including positive emotions such as excitement, joy, and curiosity, in order to facilitate the wanting of reward.

Building Positivity

Chapter 7 presents a set of experiential skills designed to cultivate and savor positive experiences that are intended to increase the liking of reward. These skills include daily practices of the mental act of giving through the practice of *Loving-Kindness* (i.e., mentally sending thoughts of happiness, health, peace, and freedom from suffering) and the physical act of giving through *Generosity* (i.e., engaging in an act of generosity at least once daily without expecting return). They also involve daily practices of the mental act of wishing continued fortune to others through *Appreciative Joy* (i.e., wishing continued health, joy, and fortune) and of generating a sense of gratefulness through the practice of *Gratitude*. Mood is rated before and after each exercise to evaluate the mood-inducing effects; doing so also targets the learning of reward (i.e., by engaging in this practice, mood improves).

Much of the content of this chapter was adapted from loving-kindness, generosity, appreciative joy, and gratitude practices developed at the UCLA Mindful Awareness Research Center. We modified these techniques so that the exercises focused only on positive aspects.

The skill of *Loving-Kindness* has been described as an act of training one's emotional experience toward warmth and tenderness (Garland et al., 2010). It is a skill that encourages the practitioner to focus awareness on loving and kind concern of other living beings, oneself, and the world (Hofmann et al., 2011). It is thought to be particularly helpful for alleviating strong negative emotions such as hostility, anger, self-criticism, and shame through increases in empathy and positive mood. Practices in *Loving-Kindness*, even brief ones (Hutcherson et al., 2008), have been shown to lead to increases in positivity toward self and others and improvements in positive affect and personal resources (e.g., personal relationship with others, physical health, self-acceptance, satisfaction) (Fredrickson et al., 2008). Preliminary evidence from proof-of-concept clinical trials in individuals with schizophrenia (Mayhew & Gilbert, 2008), posttraumatic stress disorder (Kearney et al., 2013), and dysthymia (Hofmann et al., 2015) show increases in positive emotions and an improved sense of self and others.

Acts of *Generosity* similarly have been linked to improvements in positive mood (Nelson et al., 2016; Rowland & Curry, 2019). In a reciprocal cycle, prosocial behaviors have been shown to increase positive mood, which in turn increases prosocial behaviors (Snippe et al., 2018). Furthermore, there is some evidence that the positive mood effects of prosocial behavior toward others are greatest for those with depression, at least in adolescent samples (Schacter & Margolin, 2019).

Cultivating *Gratitude* (by creating gratitude lists, gratitude contemplation, or the behavioral expression of gratitude) leads to state changes in positive mood, greater resourcefulness, and general well-being (Froh et al., 2009; Geraghty et al., 2010a, 2010b; Wood et al., 2010), albeit in nonclinical samples. It is speculated that practicing *Gratitude* leads to increased value of help from others (Maltby et al., 2008; Wood et al., 2010), which leads to seeking more social support and strengthening social bonds (Wood et al., 2008a). This "broaden and build" approach (Fredrickson, 2001) is thought to add to resiliency (Emmons & McCullough, 2003).

Appreciative Joy is a practice that involves feeling happiness for people with success, good fortune, or happiness. Similar to practices of *Loving-Kindness*, *Appreciative Joy* has been associated with increases in positive mood, positive thinking, interpersonal relations, empathic accuracy, and improvements in psychological distress, although studies have limitations (Shonin et al., 2015; Zeng et al., 2015). In one small study, *Appreciative Joy* alone was found to increase positive mood in a healthy sample (Zeng et al., 2019).

General Treatment Format and Guiding Therapy Principles

(Corresponds to chapter 3 of client workbook)

Treatment Module and Schedule Overview

As mentioned in chapter 2, the Positive Affect Treatment (PAT) was developed with theory, science, and clinical experience in mind. PAT follows the rationale, components, and structure of traditional evidence-based therapies. At the same time, it encourages tailoring to the clients' needs and priorities (see p. 32 later in this chapter). Flexibility is of the essence as individuals with anhedonia (low positive affect) are lacking the prerequisites for cognitive–behavioral therapy to be successful: motivation! The very nature of anhedonia is lack of drive, motivation, and ability to enjoy or appreciate positive change, at least at first. Those deficits need to be carefully considered, and treatment should be adjusted accordingly to ensure maximum client benefits.

The early part of treatment focuses on actions and behavioral change. Research suggests that early behavioral change is associated with early-in-treatment therapeutic gains. In PAT, behavioral change is designed to increase reward sensitivity and access to rewards in the environment that in turn reinforces further behavioral change. Those gains are essential to motivation and drive. Behavioral gains are then complemented by cognitive changes and positive practices designed to build reward capacity even further. Behavioral changes are not the focus of the second half of treatment but should continue nonetheless as the new cognitive and positive practice skills are targeted.

As is standard in evidence-based psychotherapy, everyday practice is a fundamental ingredient of this therapy.

Module Summaries

Module 1: Psychoeducation

- Duration: One or two sessions
- Corresponding therapist guide chapter: 1, 2, 3, 4
- Corresponding client workbook chapters: 1, 2, 3, 4

This module was designed to provide psychoeducation on the nature of anhedonia, therapy expectations and structure, and the concepts of the mood cycle. Clients are educated about the nature of anhedonia, the consequences of anhedonia, associated psychiatric conditions, and the efficacy of PAT. They are also presented with the basic principles of the treatment format and expectations, and they are given an opportunity to determine their readiness and need for treatment. At this point in treatment, the therapist should consider treatment tailoring (chapter 3). Clients are then introduced to the interrelationship of thoughts, behaviors, and physical sensations or feelings (the mood cycle) and how they are targeted in PAT. They will also learn what an upward spiral is, as opposed to a downward spiral, and how it influences how we think, act, and feel. Clients practice their own example of a positive mood cycle.

Next, clients are introduced to different types of positive emotions through labeling (using the labeling emotions exercise). Clients learn that identifying and labeling the different positive emotions requires careful attention and increases positive affect. They are given the opportunity to review and individualize a positive label chart.

Module 2: Treatment Skill Sets: Actions Toward Feeling Better

- Duration: Six sessions
- Corresponding therapist guide chapter: 5
- Corresponding client workbook chapter: 5

The key concepts in this chapter are to increase engagement in positive activities, examine the relationship between behavior and mood, and savor the positive moments. Clients are instructed in the importance of doing positive activities, how to increase the frequency of positive activities, and how to experience positive emotions more intensely in those activities. To achieve this goal, clients begin by reviewing a list of positive activities and mastery activities. They then create their own positive activity list. They conduct mood recording to identify which activities generate more positive emotions in their everyday lives. Then, clients schedule positive activities, followed by a *Savoring the Moment* exercise that aims to enhance the memory of the most rewarding aspect of the activity.

Module 2: Treatment Skill Sets: Attending to the Positive

- Duration: Three sessions
- Corresponding therapist guide chapter: 6
- Corresponding client workbook chapter: 6

The key concepts in this chapter are to increase one's ability to notice positive aspects of situations, to anticipate positive outcomes, and to take responsibility for one's own contribution to positive outcomes. These are achieved by a set of thinking skills, including *Finding the Silver Linings*, *Taking Ownership*, and *Imagining the Positive*. In *Finding the Silver Linings*, clients are asked to identify and appreciate positive aspects in everyday situations, no matter how negative they may seem. *Taking Ownership* skills are aimed at shifting the client's attention toward their own positive contribution to a positive event in their lives.

Imagining the Positive involves repeatedly imagining positive outcomes in an upcoming event.

Module 2: Treatment Skill Sets: Building Positivity

- Duration: Four sessions
- Corresponding therapist guide chapter: 7
- Corresponding client workbook chapter: 7

This chapter involves a set of experiential skills designed to cultivate and savor positive experiences. Through daily practices of mental giving (*Loving-Kindness*), physical acts of giving (*Generosity*), *Gratitude,* and wishing well (*Appreciative Joy*), clients are given the opportunity to cultivate positive emotions toward themselves and others. They allow clients to shift their focus away from negative emotions such as self-hatred, anger, shame, or disappointment toward positive emotions such as empathy, self-acceptance, and satisfaction.

Module 3: Treatment Gains and Relapse Prevention

- Duration: One session
- Corresponding therapist guide chapter: 8
- Corresponding client workbook chapter: 8

The final module reviews progress, establishes a practice plan, and provides guidance on ways of dealing with challenging times and barriers in the future, in order to maintain gains and minimize relapse.

Treatment Schedule

Figure 3.1 provides an overview of the recommended treatment schedule and structure. As discussed later in this chapter (see p. 32), as the therapist, you may wish to change the order and duration of sessions depending on the client's reward sensitivity deficits and resources (e.g., time).

Week	Chapter	Title
1	1-4	**Assessment** ▪ *Exercise 2.1: Treatment Fit Assessment* ▪ *Exercise 2.2: Treatment Timing Assessment* **Psychoeducation on Anhedonia and Treatment Overview** **The Mood Cycle** ▪ *Exercise 4.1: A Mood Cycle You Noticed* **Labeling Emotions** ▪ *Exercise 4.2: Positive Emotions Dial* **Actions Toward Feeling Better** ▪ *Exercise 5.1: Daily Activity and Mood Record*
2	5	**Actions Toward Feeling Better** ▪ *Exercise 5.1: Daily Activity and Mood Record* ▪ *Exercise 5.2: Positive Activity List* ▪ *Exercise 5.3: Positive Activity List through Mastery* ▪ *Exercise 5.4: My Positive Activity List*
3	5	**Actions Toward Feeling Better** ▪ *Exercise 5.5: Positive Activity Scheduling*
4-7	5	**Actions Toward Feeling Better** ▪ *Exercise 5.5: Positive Activity Scheduling* ▪ *Exercise 5.6: Savoring the Moment*
8	6	**Attending to the Positive** ▪ *Exercise 6.1: Finding the Silver Linings*
9	6	**Attending to the Positive** ▪ *Exercise 6.2: Taking Ownership*
10	6	**Attending to the Positive** ▪ *Exercise 6.3: Imagining the Positive*
11	7	**Building Positivity** ▪ *Exercise 7.1: Practicing Loving-Kindness*
12	7	**Building Positivity** ▪ *Exercise 7.2: Gratitude*
13	7	**Building Positivity** ▪ *Exercise 7.3: Generosity*
14	7	**Building Positivity** ▪ *Exercise 7.4: Appreciative Joy*
15	8	**Continuing the Journey on Your Own** ▪ *Exercise 8.1: My Progress Assessment* ▪ *Exercise 8.2: My Long-Term Goals* ▪ *Exercise 8.3: Maintaining My Gains* ▪ *Exercise 8.4: Overcoming Barriers*

Figure 3.1

Recommended treatment schedule.

PAT is administered face to face in an individual format. Like most other evidence-based psychotherapies, clients can meet with their therapists weekly for 50 to 60 minutes. The recommended standard therapy duration is 15 weeks, and program modifications can be considered (see "Program Adaptations" later in this chapter). The order, layout, and structure follow cognitive–behavioral treatments, including those in the Treatments *That Work*™ series.

Exercise Forms

We designed exercises to be used daily throughout the program that are easy for therapists to explain and for clients to use. Each exercise is first completed in session with the therapist before the client uses it for home practice. Make sure that your clients are provided with enough copies of the exercise forms for their daily practices at home. Your clients and you may photocopy all exercises from the client workbook or download multiple copies at the Treatments *That Work*™ website (www.oxfordclinicalpsych.com/PAT).

Encourage your clients to review the exercise instructions before starting an exercise at home to ensure that they practice each skill as intended. The assignments require clients to rate their mood before and after each activity or practice, using a 0-to-10-point scale, where 0 stands for "lowest mood" while 10 stands for "highest mood". Those ratings are a fundamental part of mood improvement tracking. They allow therapists to determine whether an activity works or not. If an activity or event does not result in improvements in mood, modifications may need to be made (see the "Troubleshooting" suggestions for each skill). The mood ratings also provide valuable feedback, encouragement, and a sense of accomplishment to the clients, who by the very nature of anhedonia struggle to notice or feel positive emotions.

Exercises should be completed as instructed. Importantly, you can model writing responses on the exercise forms to increase the chances of client compliance. Clients sometimes complete forms retrospectively, after having done the exercises. Yet, retrospective recollection of their exercises and mood will likely be affected by negative biases in attention and memory, characteristic of anxiety and depression. Furthermore, retrospective recollection means that information about in-the-moment mood changes will get lost. Lastly, the act of writing has multiple benefits in and of itself, including "slowing the mind." Individuals with anxiety or depression often report that their "minds are racing" or that they are easily "distractible." Writing can focus attention and in turn facilitate encoding and memory consolidation about positive, rewarding experiences that would otherwise be dismissed.

Homework

As for any evidence-based intervention, regular homework practice is essential. Skills within each section are intended to be practiced daily (typically one exercise per day) for the recommended time (e.g., one week) that we provide. Practice is encouraged no matter how simple or easy the skills seem to the client. Repeated practice builds mastery and is necessary to transform the skills into habits.

Of course, if clients already have mastered specific skills, consider the program modifications outlined later in the chapter. Likewise, if more time is needed, extend the amount of time to practice with exercises before moving on to the next chapter. Lastly, remember that the skills training from one section of a skill set (e.g., Actions Toward Feeling Better) should be carried over into the next skill set (i.e., Attending to the Positive), if clinically indicated.

Some skills will be best practiced regularly at the beginning or end of each day (e.g., *Finding the Silver Linings, Imagining the Positive, Gratitude, Loving-Kindness, Appreciative Joy*). In contrast, others will be best practiced when scheduled during the day (e.g., *Practicing Positive Activities, Taking Ownership, Generosity*). Remind clients to avoid pushing their practices to the end of the day, when low drive and motivation may become stronger impediments.

Assessment and Monitoring

Mental health professionals may wish to screen clients for the presence of emotional disorders using the Anxiety Disorders Interview Schedule for DSM-5 (Brown & Barlow, 2021), which was designed for this purpose. The semi-structured diagnostic clinical interview focuses on DSM-5 diagnoses of anxiety disorders and their accompanying mood states, somatoform disorders, and substance and alcohol use. For a fuller diagnostic picture, including a more in-depth evaluation of the various mood disorders and psychoses, you may consider using the SCID-5 (First et al., 2016). The information derived from these interviews allows you to determine differential diagnoses and to gather a clear understanding of the level of severity of each diagnosis. A medical evaluation may be appropriate to rule out medical conditions that may account for or exacerbate anhedonia.

A number of standardized self-report inventories can be very useful for case formulation and treatment planning, as well as evaluating therapeutic change. For direct measures of affect, the Positive and Negative Affect Schedule (PANAS; Watson et al., 1988) provides state and trait measures of mood state, again with strong psychometric properties. For assessment of symptoms of depression and anxiety, we often use the Depression, Anxiety and Stress Scale (DASS; Lovibond & Lovibond, 1995). This scale has excellent psychometric properties. We strongly recommend that you have clients complete both scales at the beginning of each treatment session to assess ongoing progress and determine treatment success (see chapter 8 in this guide).

For anhedonic symptoms in particular, the Temporal Experience of Pleasure Scale (Gard et al., 2006) (anticipatory and consummatory subscales) provides psychometrically valid measures of reward responsiveness. Similarly, the Snaith-Hamilton Pleasure Scale (Snaith et al., 1995) measures hedonic capacity with good psychometric characteristics. The Dimensional Anhedonia Rating Scale (Rizvi et al., 2015) measures aspects of interest, motivation, and effort related to reward responsiveness, again with good psychometric properties.

Therapists may also find it valuable to examine functional impairment and quality of life. A number of reliable and validated measures exist, including the Work and Social Adjustment Scale (Mundt et al., 2002), which is perhaps most widely used in clinical settings.

Program Adaptations

Although PAT was tested and studied in the format described earlier in the chapter (i.e., 15 individual, weekly sessions) adaptations can be made. For example, now with improvements in technology, PAT can be offered virtually over telehealth platforms. This may allow for greater access.

Frequency

If schedules of the client and therapist permit twice-a-week appointments, then treatment can be offered twice a week for an eight-week duration. Therapists might opt for this schedule if their client is of higher risk or if time is limited. For higher-functioning clients with limited availability for weekly sessions, offering sessions every two to three weeks may still be beneficial for the client, if they practice their skills regularly between sessions.

Duration

Treatment duration can be tailored to the client's needs. It can be abbreviated or extended. For example, clients may need fewer sessions devoted to the skills covered in chapter 5 (Actions Toward Feeling Better) if they are already effectively engaging in positive activities. Conversely, you can spend an additional session on certain skills that seem to require more practice. However, we generally aim to complete the program within 15 sessions.

Tailoring Treatment

In addition to tailoring treatment based on client severity (e.g., greater severity might require more frequent sessions or spending more time on certain skills), treatment can be tailored to client-specific reward system deficits. If a client demonstrates strengths in one area of the reward system but limitations in another, then you can adapt the therapy to spend more time on the skills that target the limitations. Recall that we focus on three main components of the reward system: anticipation and motivation for reward (wanting), attainment or savoring of reward (liking), and learning of reward. If a client demonstrates deficits in anticipation of reward, more time can be spent on *Designing Positive Activities* and on *Imagining the Positive*. If clients struggle with learning of reward, it may be beneficial to focus on *Taking Ownership*, *Gratitude*, and *Generosity* earlier in treatment. For clients who struggle with attainment of reward, then *Practicing Positive Activities, Savoring the Moment, Loving-Kindness, and Appreciative Joy* should be more strategically targeted.

We provide a list of questions in the client workbook to identify where clients have the most deficits or difficulties with respect to aspects of reward processes (anticipation and motivation, attainment, and learning). These questions can be found in Exercise 2.1: Treatment Fit Assessment, which is in the client workbook and also in the appendix at the end of this therapist guide.

Group Versus Individual Format

The treatment can be adapted from individual to group format, and in fact we have conducted PAT in group formats. Ideally groups would be about eight to 12 members. For group formats, therapists can follow the same recommended schedule as treatment offered in an individual format.

Involving Family Members and Friends

The extent of family and friend involvement should depend on client preference and context. Have a thorough discussion with your clients around how they wish to include loved ones and issues that may arise, which could become barriers to implementing the treatment. It is important to stress that even with family involvement, the client remains the client. Also, a Release of Information or Authorization to Disclose will be required in many circumstances.

At minimum, we recommend that clients share their involvement in therapy with supportive loved ones. We acknowledge that in certain unhealthy relationships, disclosure of treatment engagement may not be safe or prudent. Having loved ones be supportive increases the likelihood of client engagement and may even improve treatment outcomes. Ideally, the client will share the skills they are learning with loved ones after each session.

Client Commitment

Like all other evidence-based treatments, client engagement is essential. Clients need to be actively engaged in session when learning, practicing, and reviewing skills, as well as at home when completing homework. Although skills need not be practiced daily, daily practice will improve treatment outcome. Recommendations for frequency of practice are provided with each skill and associated exercises. Standard motivational enhancement techniques (e.g., reviewing treatment goals, assessing and troubleshooting barriers, reviewing consequences, and reinforcing participation) can facilitate engagement. If a client demonstrates insufficient engagement (e.g., minimal homework completion) for multiple weeks, we recommend that you put the treatment on hold until the client is able to commit to the treatment.

| CHAPTER 4 | Psychoeducation |

(Corresponds to chapter 4 of client workbook)

Materials Needed

- Whiteboard or a piece of paper to draw out the mood cycle
- Exercise 4.1: A Mood Cycle You Noticed (all exercises are included in the client workbook and also included in the appendix at the end of this therapist guide)
- Exercise 4.2: Positive Emotions Dial

Goals

- Introduce the mood cycle and have the client record one of their own mood cycles using Exercise 4.1.
- Explain upward and downward cycles.
- Introduce Exercise 4.2: Positive Emotions Dial and the importance of labeling emotions.
- Help clients identify additional positive emotions to include on the exercise form.
- Assign homework of recording a mood cycle and identifying positive emotions.

Summary of Information in Chapter 4 of the Client Workbook

- The mood cycle explains what leads to emotions and what emotions lead to.
- How we think (thoughts), what we do (behavior), and how our body feels (physical sensations) can directly change how we feel (emotions/mood). Our emotions or mood can change how we think, what we do, and how our body feels. Further, thoughts, behaviors, and physical sensations all affect each other.
- Together, thoughts, behaviors, and physical sensations form the mood/emotion cycle.
- There are positive and negative mood cycles, and there are downward and upward spirals.
- Upward spirals, like downward spirals, are self-perpetuating mood cycles.
- The goal of this treatment is to help clients step into upward spirals.
- There is an array of positive emotions beyond happiness.
- Labeling the full array of positive emotions increases attention to and experiences of positivity.
- The goal of this treatment is to enhance the diversity, frequency, and intensity of positive emotions.

Key Concepts

The key concepts of this chapter are the introduction of the mood cycle, upward spirals, labeling emotions, and the variety of positive emotions one can experience. Content can be covered in one session. Clients will learn what mood cycles are and how to identify them, as well as how to label their positive emotions throughout the week. Goals for the client are:

- Define a mood cycle
- Identify a positive or negative mood cycle from their week
- Define what an upward spiral is and how it relates to the skills they will learn in this treatment
- Expand client vocabulary of positive emotions
- Label positive emotions in the coming week

What Is the Mood Cycle?

The mood cycle describes the relationship between mood/emotion, thoughts, behaviors, and physical sensations (Figure 4.1). Each of these constructs influences each other, with thoughts, behaviors, and physical sensations being conceptualized as three parts of mood/emotion. Thoughts affect emotions; physical sensations affect emotions; behaviors affect emotions; and these relationships are bidirectional. Note too that thoughts, behaviors, and physical sensations—the triad of emotions—also affect each other, forming a cycle with relationships in all directions.

Mood cycles can be positive or negative. Positive mood cycles are cycles with positive mood/emotions at the center, whereas negative mood cycles are those with negative emotions at the center. Most people come to therapy in the hope of changing their mood or physical symptoms. The mood cycle demonstrates that we can indirectly change how we feel by working with our thoughts and behaviors. This is the cognitive–behavioral approach that the Positive Affect Treatment (PAT) uses. In this treatment, clients learn thinking skills and behavioral skills to indirectly change how they feel. In order for the client to understand key concepts in this treatment, reviewing the mood cycle is essential. Often clients struggle to differentiate between these internal experiences, confusing a thought with an emotion or an emotion with a physical

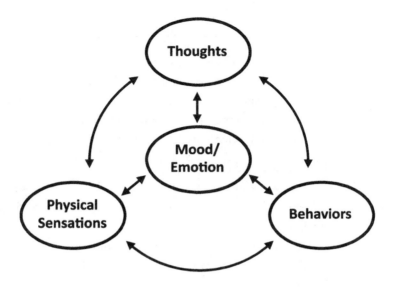

Figure 4.1

The mood cycle.

symptom. Further, many clients are not aware of the relationship between these constructs. Therefore, review the model with exemplars of how emotions will shift depending on appraisals of a given situation. Common examples are a friend passes us by without saying hello or a sound wakes us up in the middle of the night. The former situation is used in the client workbook.

When walking through an example, writing down the client's answers on a whiteboard or piece of paper (similar to what is drawn in the workbook on pages 32–35) can help the client better visualize the connection between emotions/mood, thoughts, physical symptoms, and behaviors.

Below is an example of how you might introduce the mood cycle. Note that T and C represent "Therapist" and "Client" in the following example.

T: *I'd like to start us off today with an exercise. Let's take the hypothetical situation that a friend passes you by without saying "hello." What might be some thoughts running through your head?*

C: *My friend didn't see me. Or, my friend is angry at me because of something I did.*

T: *Okay, great. Let's go with the thought that your friend is angry at you for something you did wrong. If you believe that you friend is angry at you for what you did wrong, what would you feel?*

C: *I would feel bad.*

T: *For sure. Maybe you would feel some guilt?*

C: *Yes.*

T: *Okay, so let's draw an arrow from the thought "My friend is angry at me for something I did" to the emotion of guilt.* [See Figure 4.2.]

Figure 4.2

An example of a negative thought leading to a negative emotion.

T: *Now, if you felt guilt, what do you think you would feel in your body? Tension anywhere?*

C: *Yes, probably a heaviness and difficulty making eye contact.* [See Figure 4.3.]

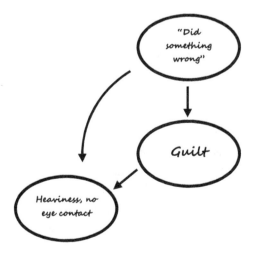

Figure 4.3

An example of a negative thought and negative emotion leading to physical symptoms.

T: Let's add that. And what would you do if you felt guilt or thought you did something wrong?

C: I would call my friend and apologize.

T: Okay, let's write that down. What are you noticing here? [See Figure 4.4.]

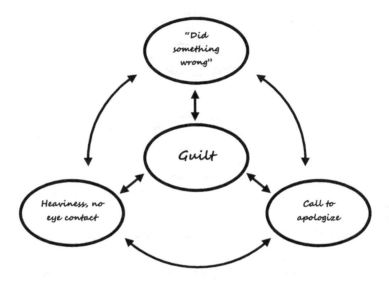

Figure 4.4

An example of the full mood cycle.

C: They are all connected, like a circle.

T: Absolutely! They form a cycle. We call this the mood cycle, with mood or emotions in the center. We like to think of mood as having three parts—thoughts, behaviors, and physical sensations—which not only influence mood but also influence each other.

C: This makes a lot of sense.

T: Let's go over another example, but this time, you think, "That Bryan. He always has his head in the clouds, probably thinking about the next song he's going to write." What emotions and physical symptoms do you think you would feel then?

C: I would probably chuckle a little and smile. I am not sure what emotion though.

T: Would you possibly feel amusement?

C: That sounds about right.

T: What would you do?

C: *I would probably call him and make a little fun of him for being so oblivious he didn't even say hi.*

T: *Absolutely. Notice how the mood cycle fits even for positive emotions.*

After introducing the mood cycle, have clients complete their own version, preferably one they noticed during the past week. It can be positive or negative, or they can complete a mood cycle for each. Given anhedonia, clients will struggle most with generating a positive mood cycle. They can record these mood cycles on Exercise 4.1: A Mood Cycle You Noticed, which appears in the client workbook and also in the appendix at the end of this therapist guide.

In sum, the following concepts should be covered with the client:

- *Thoughts → emotions*: How we interpret or think about a situation directly affects how we feel.
- *Behaviors → emotions*: What we do has a direct effect on how we feel. One way to highlight this concept is to ask the client what emotions they feel when doing their least-liked activity versus their favorite activity.
- *Physical sensations → emotions*: Physical sensations or symptoms also influence our emotions. Provide clients with examples of how they feel with physical pain versus no pain.
- *Mood/emotions*: Things that we think, do, and feel physically affect our mood and can be thought of as parts of mood.
- Thoughts, behaviors, and physical sensations all have an effect on our emotions. The reverse is also true: Our mood and emotions affect what we think, do, and feel in our body.
- Finally, each part of the mood triad affects other parts of mood—they are interconnected.
- In this treatment, we are having clients learn thinking skills and behavioral skills to indirectly change how they feel.

Downward and Upward Spirals

Downward spirals are self-perpetuating cycles of negative emotion, which are maintained by negative thoughts and behaviors (Garland et al., 2010). For example, a negative thought leads to another negative thought, which leads to a negative emotion, which leads to more negative thoughts. These negative thoughts lead to problematic behaviors, which maintain the negative emotion and fuel the negative thoughts. Notice how these spirals are an extension of the mood cycle we just described.

Most therapists have countless examples of downward spirals that their clients present with. However, less recognized are upward spirals. *Upward spirals* follow the same pattern as downward spirals, but instead of maintaining negative emotion, they maintain positive emotions (Garland et al., 2010). Upward spirals were first identified following research that demonstrated an association between current and future positive experiences (Fredrickson & Joiner, 2002). Other research since then has demonstrated that experiencing positive emotions facilitates cognitive reappraisal (Tugade & Fredrickson, 2004). It dampens attentional biases toward the negative (Smith et al., 2006), and broadens attention and builds resources (Fredrickson, 2001).

A primary goal of PAT is to help clients step into upward spirals by practicing skills that have been proven to predict positive emotions.

In sum, the following should be covered with clients:

- Upward and downward spirals as self-maintaining systems
- Effect of upward spirals on positive emotions, appraisals, attention, and resources
- Client's experience of upward or downward spirals in the last week
- How upward and downward spirals are an extension of the mood cycle
- How these spirals relate to skills in this treatment (i.e., the intention of skills is to help clients step into upward spirals)

Labeling Emotions

Individuals who are depressed can have difficulty labeling emotions (alexithymia) (Honkalampi et al., 2001). Since people with anhedonia experience fewer positive emotional states overall, their repertoire for describing positive emotions is typically limited. Building repertoire requires discriminating among different strengths and types of positive emotions (e.g., joy, thrill, contentment), and such discrimination facilitates attention to and encoding of internal states (e.g., physical sensations, thoughts) associated with each positive emotion. Training to attend to internal states associated with hedonic feelings offsets the deficits in sustained attention to positive stimuli that characterizes depression and anhedonia (Shane & Peterson, 2007), with a preference to attend to negative stimuli (Koster et al., 2005). Hence, the process of labeling positive emotions is likely to enhance attention to positive experiences that will increase the attainment of reward.

For these reasons, labeling positive emotions is introduced as a skill. Clients typically have a more varied vocabulary for negative emotions than positive emotions. Indeed, clients often struggle to identify any positive emotions beyond love or happiness. Part of this section is to expand the positive emotion vocabulary of clients, who will then use these feeling words to label their emotional experience throughout treatment. Another purpose of this skill is to help clients more accurately label their emotions to increase the salience of their emotions.

To introduce the exercise, we use Exercise 4.2: Positive Emotions Dial, which can be found in the client workbook and also in the appendix at the end of this therapist guide. The dial is designed so that clients can see that there is not only a variety of positive emotions, but that they vary in intensity too. For example, satisfaction is a lower level of intensity than happiness, which in turn is lower in intensity than elation.

Having the client read through the various positive emotions and discuss their reactions can start a helpful dialogue around their current experience with positive emotions. If there are some positive emotions that clients already experience, they can annotate it on the chart. If they notice some positive emotions missing from the chart, they can add more. Finally, clients can star, circle, or underline any emotions that resonate most with them.

Homework

Clients may photocopy exercises from the workbook or download multiple copies at the Treatments *That Work*™ website (www. oxfordclinicalpsych.com/PAT). For homework, ask your clients to:

- Complete one full Exercise 4.1: A Mood Cycle You Noticed for an event over the next week.
- Practice identifying and labeling positive emotions.

- Add additional positive emotions they might notice missing from Exercise 4.2: Positive Emotions Dial.

Case Vignettes

Note that T and C represent "Therapist" and "Client" in the following case vignettes.

Case Vignette #1

In the following vignette, the therapist has introduced the mood cycle and downward and upward spirals. The client is now asking follow-up questions for clarification.

C: *Okay, so I definitely understand what negative mood cycles are. I have them all the time. I even see how they relate to downward spirals. For example, just yesterday, I had the thought, "My boss is going to fire me." This led me to feel incredibly anxious, which made me really nauseous. So I decided to take the day off. But all I did then was lie in bed watching TV all day and worrying more. And that made me feel more anxious and sick. Now today, I have so much work to do that I actually feel worse now than I did yesterday.*

T: *It seems like yesterday and today have been really rough for you. I am sorry to hear that.*

C: *Yes, it hasn't been great.*

T: *But it also sounds like you have a really good understanding of these concepts and are spot on at identifying your own negative mood cycles and downward spirals.*

C: *I mean, I get all that. I am just not sure I understand positive mood cycles and upward spirals.*

T: *Well, then, let's definitely talk more about them. I would like to understand better what specifically about them is holding you up right now. Let's start with the positive mood cycle. Is there something specific about the positive mood cycle that you are confused about?*

C: *No, just everything.*

T: Okay, then let's tackle everything. Since you understand the concept of a mood cycle more generally, especially a negative mood cycle, let's start with what makes a mood cycle positive versus negative.

C: Okay, I think I know this. A positive mood cycle is just one that makes you feel good.

T: Generally, yes. A positive mood cycle includes positive emotions or emotions that we enjoy, like love, interest, excitement, and joy, whereas, a negative mood cycle is one that includes negative emotions or emotions that we typically don't like to have—like anxiety, sadness, and anger.

C: I guess I get all that. What I don't get is what that looks like for me. How can a positive emotion lead me to feel good in my body or lead me to do an action?

T: Great questions. The best way to answer is by going over an example. Drawing it out can really help, too, so as we go through the example, I will be drawing it out on the whiteboard.

C: Okay. Should I also record this on my workbook exercise form?

T: That would be a great idea. Do you have an example from the past day or week when you felt a positive emotion, like contentment, satisfaction, love, excitement, curiosity, interest, amusement, or pride?

C: Well, definitely not pride. And I don't know the last time I felt any happiness. Hmm (thinking). What were those positive emotions again?

T: Interest, curiosity, amusement, excitement, love, satisfaction . . .

C: I guess I feel love. I don't feel it strongly anymore, but I know it's there.

T: Fantastic. And when was the last time you actually felt the emotion, rather than just knowing it was there?

C: The last time I felt love? Hmm, well, the last time I felt it was almost two months ago. My daughter got accepted to her dream college. She wants to become an engineer for NASA. I felt like my heart was going to burst, I felt so much love for her.

T: Wow, congratulations! That is such an accomplishment. It sounds like you may have also felt some pride for your daughter.

C: Pride? No, it wasn't me who got her into her dream college. It was all her. She is incredible.

T: Well, if not pride, then some happiness for her?

C: I definitely felt happiness for her.

T: When she opened the email and you felt this love and happiness for her, what did you feel physically in your body?

C: I don't know. Nothing, I think.

T: Well, even now as you describe your daughter opening her acceptance email, I see some changes in your face. What are those?

C: A smile, I guess. (laughter)

T: Absolutely. What else?

C: I feel some tears too.

T: I notice that as well. Maybe they are some tears of joy or love?

C: Yea, definitely. (client sniffles)

T: Let's add all of this to the mood cycle. Love and joy lead to smile and tears. Can you now see how a positive emotion might lead to a change in physical sensations?

C: Yes. So is a smile a physical sensation or a behavior?

T: Great question. When it's automatic or involuntary, it's considered a physical sensation. However, if it is something that we consciously decide to do, then it's an action or behavior. That means that a smile can either be a physical sensation or behavior, depending on whether we are voluntarily doing it.

C: I see.

T: Speaking of behavior, what did you do after feeling that love and happiness for your daughter?

C: I just gave her a big hug and whispered in her ear how much I love her and how happy I was that she got into her dream college.

T: That sounds like it was a really loving moment.

C: It was. I felt even more love after giving her that hug, and I just felt so connected to her.

T: Wow, so not only did your emotion lead to your behavior of a hug and kind words, but those behaviors led to more positive emotion.

C: Definitely. And then, I couldn't stop thinking about how my daughter is going to do so well in life. Or at least she's on the path for that. I felt really good that morning.

T: Well, let's definitely jot that down because it sounds like you just described a positive mood cycle and an upward cycle. The positive emotions you felt led to physical symptoms and a behavior, which led to more positive emotion, which led to positive thoughts, which led to a change in mood for a good portion of the day.

C: Yes, I guess that's right. Okay, I get upward spirals and positive mood cycles now.

Case Vignette #2

This is a vignette where the therapist is introducing how to label emotions to a client who has struggled with chronic depression for most of his life.

T: *We are going to work on skills to increase the variety of positive emotions you experience. In other words, to feel more than just happiness—to feel other emotions like interest, pride, gratitude, fulfillment, and elation.*

C: *Heh, elation? Yeah, not going to happen.*

T: *Can you say more about that?*

C: *I just can't remember the last time I felt anything positive, and to think that I'm going to start feeling something like elation sounds ridiculous to me.*

T: *I hear that. Elation may not be something that we can expect right now. The good news is that there are other positive emotions—like satisfaction, pleasure, curiosity, and connection—that may be more realistic. We will go over this more when we review the Positive Emotions Dial in a moment. Do you think these other emotions are more reasonable for you?*

C: *I guess so.*

T: *The other thing that I really want to stress is that this treatment was specifically designed for someone with your symptoms and your history. It has helped many people with chronic depression start feeling positive emotions again, even if it has been years since they last remember experiencing them. Does that sound more reassuring?*

C: *It does.*

T: *So to get started, let's talk about labeling emotions. Most of us can label a ton of negative emotions with minimal difficulty—like anger, frustration, annoyance, irritation, shame, and anxiety. Does that sound familiar?*

C: *Yeah, totally.*

T: *That's true for most people. Even though most people can think of lots of negative emotions, they typically struggle to think of any positive emotions other than happiness.*

C: *That also sounds like me.*

T: *To help with that, we created this figure for you to reference* (show Exercise 4.2: Positive Emotions Dial). *Let's go over this now.*

Since lack of positive emotions is inherent to anhedonia, some clients may not have an example of a positive mood cycle. If your clients cannot generate their own positive mood cycle, encourage them to identify a positive mood cycle they have noticed in a family member or friend, or even one they've seen on TV or in the movies. Have clients practice identifying any positive mood cycles—regardless of whose it is—before starting to build their own.

Some clients report that it has been years since they have experienced a positive emotion, and they express incredulity at ever being able to experience a positive emotion, let alone a variety of positive emotions. Validate their experience and reassure them that PAT was designed specifically to help them increase the intensity, frequency, and variety of positive emotions.

Some clients may get stuck on wanting only happiness and indicate they are not interested in a variety of positive emotions. In this case, emphasize that we have an array of emotions (both positive and negative) for a reason. Explain that emotions are meant to be a form of communication with others and ourselves, and that emotions also help us learn. For example, curiosity and playfulness are emotions that help us gain knowledge about the world around us.

Some clients may be fearful that they will get stuck in an upward spiral. Explain that it is not possible to get stuck in an upward spiral, unless they have a history of clinical mania. If the client does have such a history, it will be important to discuss possible triggers of manic episodes and avoid those throughout the course of treatment. Note that none of the PAT strategies can alone trigger a manic episode.

Note to Therapist About Monitoring Daily Activity and Mood

Typically, the "Actions Toward Feeling Better" skill set will be administered following the "Psychoeducation" module. If you follow this recommended order of skills, then we suggest that you introduce and assign homework from chapter 5's "Monitoring Daily Activity and Mood" section in the same session that you review the "Psychoeducation" module. The homework assignment for that section of chapter 5 is best completed before introducing the skill of *Designing Positive Activities*.

Treatment Skill Sets

CHAPTER 5

Actions Toward Feeling Better

(Corresponds to chapter 5 of client workbook)

Materials Needed

- Exercise 5.1: Daily Activity and Mood Record (all exercises are included in the client workbook and also included in the appendix at the end of this therapist guide)
- Exercise 5.2: Positive Activity List
- Exercise 5.3: Positive Activity List Through Mastery
- Exercise 5.4: My Positive Activity List
- Exercise 5.5: Positive Activity Scheduling
- Exercise 5.6: Savoring the Moment

Goals

- Review content from last session and answer any questions.
- Discuss purpose of monitoring daily activities and mood and assign for homework.
- Educate client about the importance of positive activities.
- Review list of positive activity examples and assist client in creating own list.
- Introduce positive activity exercise, complete in session, and assign 3-5 positive activities for homework for the upcoming week.
- Introduce *Savoring the Moment* exercise, complete in session using events from the prior week, and encourage self-guided savoring practice between sessions.

Summary of Information in Chapter 5 of Client Workbook

- Change in behavior directly influences how we feel and think.
- Low positive mood is often a result of insufficient pleasing or rewarding activities. Engaging in positive activities is a way to step into the upward positive mood cycle.
- The practice of planning and practicing positive activities, and then savoring the moments during those activities, will increase capacity to be interested in and motivated to do more positive activities, to

appreciate them in the moment, and to feel the positive effects. Noticing the positive effects on mood state will help clients learn that their efforts lead to rewarding outcomes.

Key Concepts

In this chapter, the concept of positive activities is introduced. Clients will learn to appreciate the direct link between behaviors and thoughts and feelings. They will learn how engaging in positive activities leads to a positive mood cycle and the upward spiral of their emotions. Clients plan their positive activities with you and then practice the skills between sessions. Use subsequent sessions to review the skills and deepen the intensity of rewarding emotions by savoring the moments through memory specificity training.

Goals for the client are to:

- Learn to identify positive activities.
- Learn about positive activity scheduling and its impact on positive emotions (the skills of *Designing Positive Activities* and *Practicing Positive Activities*).
- Learn to deepen the impact of positive activities through *Savoring the Moment*.

The Importance of Positive Activities

The goal of this chapter is to augment positive mood through repeated engagement with positive activities and *Savoring the Moment* exercises. The behavioral component of the mood cycle is purposefully introduced early in treatment. It is the focus of the first half of treatment, and should be continued during the second half of treatment, where new skills of thinking positively and building positivity are added. Research suggests that early behavioral change is associated with early-in-treatment therapeutic gains. Those gains are essential to maintain motivation and drive, particularly in individuals whose core deficit is often a lack of motivation and drive.

Positive activity scheduling is rooted in Lewinsohn's conceptualization of etiology and maintenance of depression (Lewinsohn, 1974). The core idea is that lack of positive reinforcement causes or is associated with depressive states. That is, individuals with depression engage in fewer positive activities, and if they do engage, they do not experience these activities as rewarding. Reactivation of positive behaviors has been shown to be effective in treating depression (Dimidjian et al., 2006; Dobson et al., 2008). Consistent with Lewinsohn's original model of behavioral activation, the focus in Positive Affect Treatment (PAT) is on activities with a high probability of generating positive emotions. These are activities that are inherently pleasant or rewarding, that provide a sense of accomplishment and/or mastery, or are consistent with valued actions. PAT adds another component of *Savoring the Moment* through memory specificity training to enhance hedonic impact (initial response to reward). This is essential to prevent dismissal of the positive activities as being irrelevant or unimportant. Instead, clients are trained to value the most positive elements through in-depth focusing of attention on the situational and sensory details.

By *Designing Positive Activities*, the skills taught in this chapter target deficits in anticipation of reward, or wanting. By *Practicing Positive Activities* and the savoring of the most positive moments of those activities through *Savoring the Moment*, the skills in this chapter also target the attainment and appreciation of reward, or liking. By emphasizing how positive activities change mood state, the skills also target learning of reward (i.e., what actions lead to positive outcomes).

Structure of "Actions Toward Feeling Better"

The first session of the "Actions Toward Feeling Better" chapter includes (1) rationale for positive activities and (2) guidance on daily activity and mood monitoring. After a week of daily activity and mood monitoring, the next session involves (1) reviewing the daily activity and mood monitoring, (2) developing a positive activity list, and (3) planning for positive activities. After a week of engaging in positive activities, each session thereafter involves (1) review of positive activities and (2) savoring of the most positive moments of the positive activities completed in the prior week. Clients are also encouraged to practice savoring of positive activities on their own between sessions.

While "Actions Toward Feeling Better" is the focus of the first half of PAT, encourage clients to continue engaging in positive activities and *Savoring the Moment* exercises throughout the entire treatment. Reinforce clients' continued engagement in positive activities as new skills are introduced in the second half of treatment.

Monitoring Daily Activity and Mood

The monitoring of activities prepares clients to identify which activities in their lives already improve their mood, and which ones do not. Instruct clients how to keep track of their activities and mood using Exercise 5.1: The Daily Activity and Mood Record, which can be found in the client workbook and also in the appendix at the end of this therapist guide. The mood rating used here is the same as the mood rating used throughout treatment. Mood monitoring is an important component of cognitive–behavioral therapy and PAT for several reasons. First, as described previously, clients with anhedonia report several deficits in reward responsivity, including deficits in noticing the hedonic impact of pleasant events, savoring reward, and Pavlovian and instrumental reward learning. Given that many positive activities are unlikely to result in significant shifts in positive mood for clients with anhedonia at the beginning of treatment, noticing even small changes in mood is an important component of learning to deepen the experience of reward. Second, tracking changes in mood across activities improves reward learning as clients develop awareness between engagement in specific activities and changes in mood. Therefore, before and after several activities in PAT, we ask clients to rate their mood on a scale from 0 (lowest mood) to 10 (highest mood).

After explaining the mood rating, explain the four benefits of using the Daily Activity and Mood Record:

1. It informs both therapist and client where their start point is, which is important for monitoring progress.

2. It creates a clear objective and accurate description of the client's daily activities.
3. It illustrates where the client has time for more positive activities.
4. It elucidates the relationship between activity and mood.

Ask clients to monitor all of their activities over the course of a week. Those activities include the number of hours the client sleeps, exercises, works, eats, plays, and engages in free time. Explain that daily monitoring is a better way of gauging the relationship between activities and mood state than is retrospective estimation.

Furthermore, monitoring allows evaluation of the linkage between behavioral activities and positive mood state. The recognition that certain activities enhance positive mood more than others provides motivation to repeat those activities and engage in other activities that are expected to lift mood. Explain to clients that they are unlikely to feel motivated to engage in specific activities (e.g., brushing teeth) if there were no direct benefit; explain that the same principle applies when targeting positive activities.

Review the Daily Activity and Mood Record at the subsequent session.

Homework for Monitoring Daily Activity and Mood

Clients may photocopy exercises from the workbook or download multiple copies at the Treatments *That Work*™ website (www.oxfordclinicalpsych.com/PAT). For homework, ask your clients to complete an Exercise 5.1: Daily Activity and Mood Record every day for a week as accurately and thoroughly as possible. Remind clients to monitor their mood before and after each of their activities on a scale of 0 for "lowest" to 10 for "highest" mood.

Case Vignette #1

This vignette demonstrates how to explain the purpose of activity and mood monitoring.

C: *Okay, I understand what I am supposed to do over the next week, but I just don't see how this will help me improve my mood. If at all, it probably will make me feel worse to see how little I am doing and how bad it makes me feel.*

T: *I hear your concern. I can assure you that it is a common one. Why would you want to be reminded of the things that make you feel bad? But there is a reason for what I am asking, and that is to get a baseline.*

C: *A baseline?*

T: *Let's go over an example to demonstrate what I mean. You have a daughter in high school, is that right?*

C: *Yes.*

T: *Okay, if she was getting low scores on her tests, what would be one of the first steps you would take?*

C: *I would definitely check in with her to see how she is doing.*

T: *Absolutely. You'd do some assessment. What else would you assess?*

C: *Maybe how much she is studying and how she is studying?*

T: *Absolutely! We need to know her baseline—what are her study habits—in order to figure out if changes need to be made.*

C: *Oh, I get it. Monitoring my daily activities will tell us if we need to change my activities to different activities.*

T: *Yes, and also tell us if we need to schedule more activities.*

C: *Okay, I get it. Why do I have to record it every day though? I can just tell you right now what my days are like.*

T: *There are several good reasons why it is helpful to gather this information in real time as supposed to retrospectively. Can you think of one?*

C: *Hmm . . . I am not sure.*

T: *One reason is that if you are not doing things in real time, you have to rely on memory. How accurate do you think memory is if you wait until the end of the week to remember what you did at the beginning of the week?*

C: *Horrible. I can't even remember what I did yesterday!*

T:	Absolutely. Our memories are not great. And, our memories tend to be less accurate when we are stressed, depressed, or anxious.
C:	Well, that's me.
T:	Yes, so the daily monitoring helps to keep things more accurate.

Case Vignette #2

This vignette addresses situations when clients do not complete their monitoring record.

C:	I am sorry I did not complete the record sheet.
T:	Well, let's talk more about that. Would you mind sharing the reasons why you did not?
C:	I just did not feel motivated.
T:	Okay, I can understand that. In fact, that's the issue we are targeting with this treatment.
C:	And honestly, I felt a bit embarrassed because I don't really do anything worth sharing.
T:	I totally hear that. It is very hard to share with someone, including your therapist, something that you feel embarrassed about. What are you concerned might happen if you share with me?
C:	That you will judge me for having so few activities on my record sheet.
T:	Ah, I see. Well, I can assure you that nothing you write down will lead me to think anything different of you. In fact, I am expecting there to be very few positive activities, because it is part of the reason you are here.
C:	Really?
T:	In many ways, it even helps to have a monitoring record with only a few positive activities. That means that there is a lot of room for change!
C:	(smiles and laughs a little) I guess I can see that. But isn't part of the reason I am recording my activities to see what makes me feel good?
T:	Yes, and if there aren't any of those activities, then we will add them.
C:	So other people also feel they don't do anything?
T:	Yes, but once they monitor their activities for a whole week, they are often surprised that they actually do much more than they thought they would. And some of those activities do improve their mood, even

when it is just a little bit. Why don't we fill out the form together and see what activities you remember doing yesterday and today and how they made you feel?

Troubleshooting for Monitoring Daily Activity and Mood

When reviewing the week of Daily Activity and Mood Record sheets, the goal is to reinforce how many positive activities the client completed and how many of those activities were enjoyable, emphasizing that mood increases as a function of the number of positive activities completed. The objective indicator is the increase in the mood rating. You may notice that some clients' mood is quite good already (e.g., 5 or 6 out of 10) and increases nicely (e.g., increase to 8 out of 10) after the activity. However, some clients may have a very low mood throughout most of the day(s) (e.g., 1 or 2 out of 10) and record little or no changes in mood state after the activity (e.g., increase to 3 out of 10). And in some clients, mood state may even worsen after an activity. Some clients may become self-critical because their mood ratings are low, and get stuck in the belief that an activity should be rewarding now because it was rewarding in the past. Or just because their family or friends find it rewarding, they should find it rewarding too.

Be aware of negative mood cycles and downward spirals here. In this critical, initial phase of the treatment, clients may give up because they see their lack of activities and/or enjoyment as evidence that nothing will help and nothing will change. They may even think that they are responsible for their mood state being so low or unresponsive to activities, or see it as a sign of failure. Remind your clients that the purpose of completing the *Daily Activity and Mood Record* is to determine a baseline or starting point. The goal of the treatment is to increase how much of their time is spent on pleasurable activities. In turn, this will improve their positive mood and decrease their negative mood.

The first step is to provide a therapeutic rationale for positive activities. Teach clients about how avoiding situations that have the potential to be rewarding leads to feelings of isolation and thoughts of failing. Ask clients whether they have examples of such negative cycles. You then explain how behavioral changes can change thoughts and feelings. Also explain how research has shown that clients with depression tend to withdraw from activities they previously found rewarding and how this can worsen their symptoms. Explain that reluctance to engage in potentially rewarding activities is the natural outcome from a lack of drive, motivation, or the inability to anticipate that an event will be positive, as well as the inability to derive enjoyment from the activity. The combination fuels the downward spiral. To replace this downward negative cycle with an upward positive cycle, clients will schedule 3-5 positive activities each week, and they will savor the experiences. "Feel better" behaviors or pleasurable activities promote physical and mental health and positive thoughts and feelings.

The next step is to identify activities that the client currently enjoys or has enjoyed in the past; these may also be new activities. Most importantly, the activity needs to have a high probability of increasing mood either instantaneously or soon after completion.

Present the client with examples of positive activities shown in Exercises 5.2 and 5.3; these can be found in the client workbook and also in the appendix at the end of this therapist guide. Exercise 5.2 includes examples of hedonic activities, such as taking a warm bubble bath. Exercise 5.3 includes examples that improve mood through mastery, such as meeting a deadline. Use prompting questions (e.g., *"Which of those activities do you currently enjoy?" "Which have you enjoyed in the past?" "Are there some you have always wanted to do but have never tried?"*). Instruct clients to write a C for "currently enjoy," P for "enjoyed in the past," and T for "trying out something new" next to the relevant items.

The next step is for clients to create their own positive activity list (see Exercise 5.4: My Positive Activity List, which can be found in the client workbook and also in the appendix at the end of this therapist guide). Again, this list can include things clients once found enjoyable or activities that build a sense of mastery. A good amount of activities should involve social interactions. Research has shown that social interactions are fundamental sources of positive affect (Snippe et al., 2018). Social interaction combats feelings of isolation and a lost sense of connectedness. Individuals who are depressed and withdraw from friends and loved ones are more vulnerable to hopelessness and despair.

As clients generate their own list on the exercise sheet, remind them to use items they endorsed in Exercise 5.2: Positive Activity List. You should encourage clients to add examples that bring value to their lives, such as "helping a friend" or "improving my health." Remind clients to include activities that bring immediate enjoyment or reward as well as ones that eventually will produce feelings of mastery, ownership, or contribute to valued actions (or other positive emotions) when accomplished. Activities should vary in the amount of time they take. Help the client to find a good balance between easy-to-do, quick activities such as "resting for 10 minutes with my eyes closed" to more complex ones such as "cooking dinner for a friend." All activities should be measurable.

Case Vignettes for Designing Positive Activities

Case Vignette #1

This vignette demonstrates how the therapist can handle situations where clients struggle to identify and schedule smaller activities that can be practiced daily.

T: *What do you think are some activities you can add to your activity list?*

C: *Hmm, well, I can add going on vacation. I used to love doing that. . . . I can also add celebrating holidays and birthdays with friends.*

T: *Okay, we can certainly add those to your activity lists. What are some other activities that you can do daily?*

C: *Daily? I've been wanting to write a book. I can write my book every day.*

T: *I am glad to see you are excited about the idea of going on vacation, celebrating your birthday with friends, and writing a book. I would call these "big-ticket" events. Do you know what I mean by that?*

C: *They are big things to plan for, or they don't happen often?*

T: *Exactly. Most of us love the idea of taking a break or celebrating with loved ones, and we can easily imagine that they will make us feel good. Those occasions are special because they do not happen every day. They also take a good deal of planning. But because they happen rarely and take some planning. It is important to also add activities to your list that ensure you get a frequent boost of happiness. Can you think of any of those?*

C: *Hmm . . . not really. Most of the things I do I really don't enjoy.*

T: *Are there things you have stopped doing because you felt you did not have energy for them?*

C: *Yeah, like running.*

T: *Great! Let's add that to your activity list. What about another activity that you like but have stopped?*

C: *Maybe reading a book to my son?*

T: *That sounds like a great one! Let's add that to the list.*

Case Vignette #2

This vignette demonstrates how to help clients generate items on their Positive Activity List that range in level of difficulty.

T: *Great work coming up with 10 activities! What do you notice when looking at the difficulty level?*

C: *I rated them all between a 6 and a 10.*

T: *Yes, exactly. They are rated on the high end.*

C: *Yes. Is that a problem?*

T: *It's good to have a few difficult ones on your list. And you have identified activities that have a high likelihood of generating positive emotions, and can boost your sense of mastery or connectedness.*

C: *That's what I thought.*

T: *But we also want to make sure you add activities to the list that are easy, ideally with a difficulty level below 5. Can you think of some of those?*

C: *Sure. Would doing yoga be a good example?*

T: *If it is likely to increase your positive mood, then definitely yes! What about some other ones that don't take up a lot of time and are easy to do?*

C: *I don't really know. One thing I kind of stopped doing is tending to my garden. It's easy to do and does not take much time, but somehow I have not felt motivated to do it.*

T: *That sounds like a great one to me! Let's add that one to the list too.*

Troubleshooting for Designing Positive Activities

The concept of positive activities can evoke strong hesitation. Clients may indicate that they "just don't feel like doing anything" or "just don't see the point of addressing behavior when it's the way I feel that's the problem." Such thoughts are understandable, since, by the very nature of anhedonia, clients often lack motivation and drive. They can no longer imagine that an activity "feels" good, especially when they have stopped engaging in most or especially when they derive no pleasure from them. It can also be the case that clients still enjoy activities but have trouble initiating them because they have difficulty seeing the connection between effort and outcome. Because of these inherent challenges, be validating and supportive, while indicating that the disbelief or hesitation to engage in positive activities is the very thing this treatment is designed to address.

You can assure your clients that their concerns are understable and common, while re-emphasizing that joy develops as one engages in joyful activities. Indicate that "getting started" is often the hardest part. Explain to clients the idea of the first law of inertia: "A body at rest will remain at rest, and a body in motion will remain in motion unless it is acted upon by an external force"—or, in the context of anhedonia, "Once you get in motion, it will be easier to stay in motion." You can ask clients for examples of when they thought it would be impossible to get started on something because they felt they lacked energy, the task felt overwhelming, or they just could not imagine that it would bring them any positive feelings. The goal is to find examples from the past of discovering that once clients decided to start, it was much easier to get going. The activity may have even resulted in a greater feeling of joy, sense of ownership, or accomplishment than they had anticipated.

Be prepared to repeat the therapeutic rationale for behavioral change, particularly when clients are fixated on the idea that they need to first "fix" their negative thoughts or feelings, or negative life circumstances, before they can take action. This idea can be intensified in clients who feel trapped in an adverse situation, such as a problematic partnership, a toxic work situation, or challenging living circumstances. Likewise, clients can have physical restrictions due to medical illness or other factors. It is important to listen empathically and address crises where appropriate, but to return quickly to the idea that we may not have control over many things in life but we almost always can have control over our own actions. This is a strong and hopeful message that redirects clients away from needing to "fix what's wrong before enjoying the good."

Research has shown that while cognitive–behavioral therapy successfully decreases negative mood, it is less successful in increasing positive mood. Clients treated with PAT show significant improvements in both negative and positive domains. You should remind your clients of those findings, particularly those clients who are more familiar with more traditional forms of psychosocial treatments.

For some clients, identifying current or past positive activities can be extremely difficult. Research has shown that clients who are depressed can have difficulties remembering positive events from the past. Specifically, depression is associated with deficits in generating vivid past (Werner-Seidler & Moulds, 2011) positive mental images, and devaluation of positive memories (Speer et al., 2014). As a result, they no longer imagine past activities as being joyful (even when they once used to be). Validate the client's feelings and ensure them that their experience is not uncommon. Encourage clients to think far back to activities from their childhood that they found positive (foods, outdoor activities, travel, social activities). You can also remind clients that many activities we do during the day may not necessarily feel rewarding at the moment, but they provide a sense of accomplishment or ownership soon after. Furthermore, explain that every step counts, and the smallest sense of positive emotion, even if tiny, is a step in the right direction.

It may not be difficult for some clients to list several activities, but most or all of these activities are rated as difficult to accomplish (greater than

7 on the scale of 0 to 10). This is not uncommon in clients who are severely anhedonic or depressed, since any activity feels overwhelming, even when it could be ultimately joyful and rewarding. Here again, it is important to remind the client of the law of inertia: It is the "getting into action" that is the hardest part. Encourage clients to break down the activities into easier-to-achieve ones. For instance, instead of listing "going on a run," have them consider "taking a walk around the block." It is essential that at least some activities' difficulty rating is below 5, ideally between 0 and 4.

Some clients struggle to understand why the activities should be observable. Explain that choosing activities that are observable by others or that are otherwise measurable makes it easier (and more rewarding) to monitor positive mood change. Examples such as, "I am going to try to feel better or think more positively" cannot be measured in objective, observable terms. Without measurement, it is not possible to conclude that an action was taken or to rate the mood effects of such an action. Instead, clients are prone to dissatisfaction with thoughts like, "This is never going to change."

Finally, encourage your client to avoid activities that have very little probability of being rewarding. For instance, adding "cooking dinner for a friend" to the list can be positively reinforcing if the client likes cooking. It will not be rewarding, however, if the client does not enjoy cooking. The goal is not to identify situations or events that the client avoids for reasons of fear; rather, the goal is to practice hedonic activities.

Practicing Positive Activities

Until this point, positive activities have been identified and a baseline of activities and associated mood has been established by monitoring over the span of a week. The client is now ready to start planning for and practicing positive activities. Those need to be inherently pleasurable, to provide a sense of accomplishment or mastery, or to be considered valued actions.

Emphasize how engaging in positive activities has two targets: The planning phase targets reward anticipation and motivation (or wanting), and the practice phase targets response to attainment of reward or liking. The hedonic impact is facilitated by labeling all of the positive emotions experienced during the activity. In addition, by keeping track of their mood before and after each activity, reward learning (i.e., learning that by engaging in a specific activity, positive mood increases) is also targeted.

To begin the planning phase, ask clients to choose three to five positive activities from their Positive Activity List (Exercise 5.4). The client will conduct these activities over the next week and will record them on the Exercise 5.5: Positive Activity Scheduling sheet, with one activity per exercise sheet. Clients may photocopy this exercise from the workbook or download multiple copies at the Treatments *That Work*™ website (www.oxfordclinicalpsych.com/PAT). The activities, no matter how simple they may appear, should be broken down into multiple steps, in order to minimize roadblocks at the time of activation. If the client has difficulties understanding why to break an activity down into multiple steps, ask them about skills they have learned in the past, such as learning how to drive. Did they learn to drive in just one day? No, it required multiple steps, starting with finding a driving school, signing up for lessons, learning the theory, daily practices, and so forth. Additionally, breaking down activities into manageable steps can prevent clients from feeling overwhelmed. Reassure the client that even completing some of the steps is valuable. Help the client review and write down on the Exercise 5.5 sheet the steps needed to complete their chosen activities.

Next, clients should identify in which domain an activity falls. For instance, exercising benefits health, and it can also be a leisure activity. If done with a friend, exercising would be a social activity too. Given the importance of social connectedness to emotional well-being, at least one activity domain should be a social one (i.e., with friends or family).

Ensure that the three to five activities are the right mix in terms of duration (brief vs. long) and difficulty (easy vs. difficult). If the client reports already engaging in and enjoying several positive activities, encourage the addition of activities that lead to a sense of accomplishment, value, and mastery once completed.

Ask clients to commit to a specific day(s) and time(s) of the week to do their activity and how much time they will dedicate to it, recording that information on the Exercise 5.5 sheet. Encourage the client not to overschedule as this may lead to feelings of failure.

For clients who are very low functioning, it may initially be more effective to assign only one easy-to-manage activity for practice. Choose an activity that the client can do repeatedly, such as taking a bubble bath, reading a book, or making a snack for their children. It is important to be flexible, particularly in this sensitive early phase of treatment, and capitalize on the things that the client can do, no matter how simple. For clients who are highly sensitive to perceived failure, initially choose "foolproof" activities.

Finally, remind clients to monitor their mood before and ideally right after the activity on a scale of 0 for "lowest mood" to 10 "highest mood," and label the variety of positive emotions that they experience. Ask them to keep Exercise 4.2: Positive Emotions Dial handy to facilitate this process.

Homework for Practicing Positive Activities

Clients may photocopy exercises from the workbook or download multiple copies at the Treatments *That Work*™ website (www.oxfordclinicalpsych.com/PAT). For homework, ask your clients to complete three to five positive activities each week, recording their mood before and after and labeling the full array of positive emotions experienced using Exercise 5.5: Positive Activity Scheduling.

Case Vignettes for Practicing Positive Activities

Case Vignette #1

The following vignette addresses clients who feel guilty about doing positive activities.

T: *Let's take a look at your Positive Activity Scheduling sheets. How did it go?*

C: Well . . . I was really only able to complete one activity, and even for that one, I don't think I did a good job.

T: What makes you think so?

C: I just have a really hard time doing those exercises. I am not really sure why, but it just does not feel right.

T: Would you mind elaborating a bit more?

C: Well . . . I am overwhelmed with things I should be doing—deadlines at work, stuff at home, school things for the kids, and so on. It does not feel right to indulge in a rewarding activity while letting other people down who are waiting for me to get things done!

T: I hear that. Do you feel like your brain is telling you, "The last thing you have time to do is something enjoyable?"

C: Yes, that is exactly what it is telling me!

T: And when you have this thought, how does this make you feel?

C: Just terrible!

T: And what happens to motivation when we feel terrible?

C: It evaporates. In fact, I didn't end up getting much done for work and I even picked up the kids late, because I stayed in bed too long.

T: Does this sound familiar?

C: Yeah . . . The negative mood cycle and downward spiral?

T: That's exactly right. And how do we break this cycle in this treatment?

C: We do things that make us feel better because then we feel better and are more motivated to do the other activities?

T: That's exactly right! Think about the positive activities as an energy drink or a strong cup of coffee. They make it easier to feel energized and get started on a challenging task. Even a simple, positive activity like listening to a fun song or walking in the sunlight for 10 minutes can improve your mood. And remember the law of inertia: Now you not only feel better, but you are actually "in motion," which makes it easier to keep going.

C: Yes, I guess that makes sense.

T: So how about we look over your list of activities again and see whether we can improve it. Let's make sure you have some activities that are easy to do, and maybe those you could combine with those of mastery and accomplishment. Can you think of an example?

T: I need to write an email to my daughter's teacher. Maybe I could play a fun game with my daughter and then write the email afterward?

C: That sounds like a fantastic example to me!

Case Vignette #2

This vignette provides an example of how to encourage a client who does not feel better after doing a positive activity.

C: I completed an activity almost daily, but honestly, they don't make me feel better. Sometimes I even feel worse.

T: I am sorry to hear that. Either way, I am glad that you completed the activities. As we have talked about before, getting started on regular practices is often the hardest part. You have mastered that this week. At the same time, we want these activities to make you feel better most of the time. Let's take a look at your mood ratings. What do you see?

C: Well, I guess not all of the activities were bad. Some did increase my mood, but really only slightly. For most, my mood did not change, and in some, it even got worse.

T: Okay, let's start with the positive ones. What about them do you think improved your mood?

C: Hmm . . . I am not sure, but maybe they just felt easier to do? And also, they felt good right away. Particularly walking along the beach.

T: Great! Let's make sure we keep those! Now, what about the ones that did not improve your mood or even made it worse? Did they have anything in common?

C: Well, I guess some felt a bit scary, and some were just really difficult to get started on.

T: That's a great observation. Tell me a bit more about those that felt scary or were hard to get motivated for.

C: I tried to call a friend I had not spoken to for many years. She is a really funny person, and I thought that it would be great to reconnect. I followed the first step and looked up her number, but then when I wanted to call, I got really worried that she may not want to talk to me. The thought really distracted me, and I started to feel really bad. All my motivation was gone, and it just felt like a bad idea to call her.

T: Calling someone you have not been in contact with for a while can be scary. But like with many things, we just don't know what will be the outcome until we give it a try. Unless we try, we just won't find out. And, the payoff of feeling good after can be worth it. Do you remember what we said about social activities?

C: They boost our mood more than non-social activities, even if it doesn't feel that way going into it.

T: *Exactly. Would you be willing to try calling your friend next week?*

C: *Umm, I don't know. I just wouldn't know what to say.*

T: *Fair enough. How about we role-play the conversation?*

C: *Yes, I think that would be helpful.*

Case Vignette #3

This vignette demonstrates troubleshooting with clients who only engage in the same activity.

C: *This week, the positive activity was going for a walk in my neighborhood again.*

T: *How did that go for you?*

C: *It was okay. Same as the last few weeks. I enjoy it initially because I get some fresh air and get to move around after a day of sitting at my desk at work, but it doesn't improve my mood as much as it used to.*

T: *Sometimes that can happen if we rely on something too much to boost our mood. Watching your favorite movie once in a while will probably improve your mood, but watching it on repeat every day is going to reduce how much you enjoy it. Variety is key.*

C: *I understand.*

T: *What else can you do in addition to walking to boost your mood?*

C: *Well, I have a lot on my activity list. I can choose something else from there this week.*

Troubleshooting for Practicing Positive Activities

Below we list the common challenges that clients and therapists experience with positive activities scheduling. Some issues can be directly addressed by reminding your client of the rationale for engaging in positive activities, the importance of engaging in several positive activities throughout the week, breaking them down into steps, encouraging a variety of activities in a range of difficulties, social involvement, and quality of reward (hedonic or sense of value, mastery, or accomplishment). Others will require more discussion and support. Those examples are listed here.

Activities that involve other people are highly desired and effective but often very hard for clients to do. Their negative thoughts can get in the way of their motivation and confidence to reach out to others. For those clients, role-playing can be helpful. For instance, a client may have chosen to call a long-time friend they have not spoken to for many months. Breaking the activity down into steps may not be sufficient (e.g., if the client fears they have nothing to say). The idea is not to turn the role-play into an exposure but rather to help the client find a starting point that will ultimately turn their planned activity into a successful one. In this example, the client anticipates that it will make them feel happy to reconnect. Likewise, you can facilitate activities of accomplishment and mastery through role-playing. Examples include role-playing asking for a leadership role at work or asking for help to finish a home project.

Sometimes clients report that they did not feel better after engaging in an activity. Examine whether the client was distracted or was ruminating during the activity. If so, they are unlikely to notice or appreciate the positive consequences. Here, there is value to remaining "in the moment" (i.e., mindfulness) when participating in positive activities. Another reason is that the client completed steps toward a positive activity that were not, in and of themselves, reinforcing (e.g., starting to work on a tax return or work project). In this case, positively reinforce the client's behavior and how the client feels progressing toward a given goal or value (i.e., completing the return or meeting a deadline).

Finally, be mindful of clients engaging in the same activity over and over. Encourage such clients to engage in different meaningful activities.

Activities of mastery or accomplishment can sometimes make a client feel anxious. For example, a client plans to complete an overdue project. While the activity in itself may not be rewarding, the client has determined that once it is completed, they will feel a sense of accomplishment. Such activities are important and generate positive feelings, such as pride, resilience, and joy. You should emphasize the goal of accomplishment and mastery over the anxiety experienced.

Following the first week of positive activity practice, you will teach the skill of *Savoring the Moment* through memory specificity training for an activity that the client most strongly associates with positive mood. *Savoring the Moment* training involves visualization of assigned activities, including specific sensations, thoughts, emotions, and situational details, through the first-person perspective and present tense. In brief, the therapist asks a client to recount using the present tense the positive feelings experienced in a prior week's activity. This training is designed to enhance the savoring of reward and to counteract the tendency to dismiss positive experiences and overly general memory. Specifically, clients with depression tend to struggle to generate specific memories that take place within the span of a single event or day. Without such details, the positive memory for activities can be impaired. Other memory deficits include having impoverished positive mental imagery. For instance, a client may have little problem describing past situations in a script-like way but struggles to add emotional attributes, such as feelings and sensations (e.g., what the forest smelled like, or how the client felt when seeing their child laughing). Individuals with depression also have a bias toward a third-person versus first-person perspective, which leads to less positive emotionality. Lastly, clients with depression have difficulty with valuing positive memories. The successful completion of positive activities cannot improve a client's mood if they simultaneously devalue the experience. Therefore, it is essential to actively recount the memories for such activities and increase their valuation. *Savoring the Moment* also acts as "positive attention training" that directs a client's attention to positive features of experiences.

During the *Savoring the Moment* exercises, clients visualize (preferably with their eyes closed) and recount, using the present tense, the moment-to-moment details of one of their positive activities, while highlighting the most positive moments. They are encouraged to visualize their surroundings, the emotions they felt, their physical sensations, their behaviors and their thoughts. This guided and repeated exercise is thought to deepen and help clients savor the positive aspects of their experience. If the client's attention shifts toward more negative aspects of an experience, the therapist gently redirects the client's attention toward the positive ones. By doing so, clients also learn that they have control over their attention and can shift their attention from one aspect of a situation to another. Research has shown that attention control is an effective form of emotion regulation (Gross, 1998).

Ask your client to identify an event from a completed Positive Activity Scheduling exercise sheet. This can be an activity that led to a significant improvement in their positive mood rating (e.g., from a 4 to an 8). It can also be an activity they struggled to find positive (their mood rating stayed the same or even decreased). Next, ask the client to describe the scene on Exercise 5.6: Savoring the Moment (which can be found in the client workbook and also in the appendix at the end of this therapist guide) and rate their current mood on a scale from 0 (lowest mood) to 10 (highest mood). Having the client describe the scene first is helpful as it provides an overview for the therapist. You can then use this information to guide the client to "fast forward" to more relevant details. For example, when describing a trip to the beach, a client may focus on irrelevant details during their recounting, such as the traffic during the drive to the beach. With the details provided in the overview, you will know that the majority of positive emotions and sensations occurred when the client first arrived at the beach, and you can therefore encourage the client to "fast forward" to this portion of the activity.

After completing the overview and rating their current mood, clients recount the activity with a focus on the portion of the event that elicited the strongest increase in positive mood. You can instruct clients who report no increase in positive mood to recount the event from beginning to end. You can assist the client in noticing potentially positive emotions and sensations by asking prompting questions such as, "What positive emotions do you notice?" and "Where do you feel it in your body?"

In session, clients visualize the scene in present tense. They may prefer to close their eyes during the recounting. If they do not wish to close their eyes, instruct them to soften their gaze rather than focusing directly on you. The goal is to reduce environmental distractions. Choose the format that makes it easiest for clients to stay in the present moment and experience the feelings, sensations, and thoughts they are describing. At every step of the way, remind clients to stay in visual mode, present tense, and first person whenever you notice the client moving into a more narrative style or shifting to a different topic.

Also guide your clients to slow down when they seem to be moving too quickly, in order to appreciate the moment and the experience. Asking clients to pause and sit with the physical sensations or emotions they are having can help deepen their experience of positive emotions as well. You might nudge your clients to express what they are feeling as they visualize, using observable cues (such as a smile) to prompt clients to notice their feelings. The visualization usually takes between five and 10 minutes but can take longer or shorter, and the same exercise can be repeated. However, we discourage frequent repetition of the same activity to minimize habituation of positive affect. After completing the recounting, instruct clients to rate their mood again, to evaluate the mood-inducing effects of *Savoring the Moment*. When guiding clients through the exercise for the first time, more prompts and interruptions are allowed. However, once clients repeatedly practice *Savoring the Moment* and are aware of how to engage in the exercise, therapists' prompts and interruptions should be minimal to ensure that clients stay with the imagery.

For therapists inexperienced in imaginal exercises (e.g., imaginal exposure), it is important for the client to vividly recount the activity along with the associated positive emotions, physical sensations, and thoughts. Thus, we encourage clients to close their eyes or soften their gaze, and to speak in the first person as described earlier. In addition, you may need to prompt clients to describe particular physical sensations or positive emotions to deepen their experience. When prompting clients, speak sparingly and use a soft tone of voice so as not to distract clients from the imaginal recounting. However, in the beginning, clients may have difficulty in conducting the imaginal recounting and you may have to take a more active role (see Case Vignette #1 that follows).

Case Vignettes for Savoring the Moment

Case Vignette #1

This vignette provides an example of how to conduct an imaginal recounting with a client for the first time. The therapist has to be more active to guide the client through the recounting and has to model using the first-person perspective. In addition, the therapist directs the client to repeatedly pause and "sit with" pleasant sensations.

T: *As we discussed, the purpose of Savoring the Moment is to train ourselves to notice even small increases in positive emotions, our physical sensations and thoughts during activities, and to deepen our experience of them. Now, I'd like you to recount the event of going to the beach with your friend Sarah. You mentioned that the biggest increase in your mood happened when you first arrived, right?*

C: *That's right.*

T: *Great. Start there and describe in detail what you were feeling and thinking. I'll occasionally ask some questions to help you focus on positive aspects of the situation. Now, gently close your eyes and begin to describe first arriving at the beach.*

C. *So, I was nervous that I wouldn't have anything interesting to say to Sarah because I haven't left my apartment much recently . . .*

T: *(Softly) Did you notice anything pleasant or positive as you first arrived?*

C: *Yes, the sun felt really good.*

T: *How did it feel on your body?*

C: *It felt warm.*

T: *So you are feeling the warmth of the sun . . .*

C: *I'm feeling the warmth of the sun and how warm the sand feels on my feet as we step onto the sand. We decide on a place to lay our things right by the water.*

T: *(Softly) What are you seeing right now?*

C: *The water looks so green. It feels nice to be here.*

T: *And what emotions are you feeling?*

C: *Relaxed.*

T: *So you are feeling the warmth of the sun and sand, noticing the green of the ocean, and feeling relaxed. What happens next?*

C: *Sarah and I get settled and start talking. She says how nice it is to see me. I didn't realize she missed spending time with me.*

T: *(Softly) What emotions are you feeling when she says this?*

C: *I don't know. Happy, I guess. A little sad, too.*

T: *Where do you feel the emotion of happiness in your body?*

C: *In my shoulders. I feel lighter.*

T: *I'd like you to pause right here and just sit with those sensations. Really feel them right here in this room.* (Pause for 15 seconds.) *And then what do you notice?*

Troubleshooting for Savoring the Moment

Some clients struggle with the concept of *Savoring the Moment* and how it can lead to improved reward learning. We suggest you use the description from the client workbook:

Why is *Savoring the Moment* important to do? Savoring a rewarding experience deepens your appreciation of the activity; it also deepens your experience of the positive aspects of the activity and the emotions you felt, which might otherwise be ignored or dismissed. By recounting the memory, particularly the most positive aspects of the activity, you are re-experiencing those positive aspects and strengthening learning between what you do and how you feel. In turn, that learning increases interest and preference for other positive experiences over negative experiences, all of which increases positive emotions and future involvement in positive activities.

It can be difficult to stay focused, especially in the face of tendencies to ruminate on past events or worry about future ones. All of this makes it difficult for clients to engage in an exercise that requires them to stay in the moment. Remind your client that this is a common struggle for many people, in the same way that it can be difficult to stay focused during meditation or yoga. Like those practices, this skill takes a lot of practice, and yes, clients should expect to get distracted or maybe even a bit frustrated at first. To facilitate attention during the recounting, remind clients to focus on the behavioral, emotional, and cognitive responses to the specific positive experience. Ask clients to describe in detail what they are experiencing and how they know that they are experiencing a positive emotion.

As noted above, slow down the process if you notice clients going through the exercise quickly or in narrative form. This may represent the tendency to dismiss or disconfirm leaning into the possibility of positive emotions. This is where you can guide your clients to slow down and appreciate the moment and the experience. You might nudge clients to express what they are feeling as they visualize, using observable cues (such as a smile) to prompt them to notice their feelings.

Positive body language (e.g., half-smile, not crossing arms, or open hands) can further enhance the client's ability to stay in the moment and maximize the positive emotions they are experiencing. For clients with particularly flat affect, it can be helpful to have them watch themselves discuss their activities with low affect (using a mirror or their cellphone for recording) and then watch themselves discuss the same activities as they show more affect (e.g., eyes wide open, smiling), with follow-up discussion of how their physical behavior affected their mood.

How can we ensure the emotional recounting exercise strengthens reward sensitivity? One of the best indicators is the mood rating. Did the client's mood improve as a result of *Savoring the Moment*? Another indicator is the client's ability to use the present tense when describing their experience. This is an indicator that they managed to stay in the moment. The amount of detail of the situation and the use of a range of positive words are also positive indicators. Clients' ability to re-experience their positive emotions will allow them to remember these emotions more vividly and intensely.

CHAPTER 6   Attending to the Positive

(Corresponds to chapter 6 of client workbook)

Materials Needed

- Exercise 6.1: *Finding the Silver Linings* (all exercises are included in the client workbook and also included in the appendix at the end of this therapist guide)
- Exercise 6.2: *Taking Ownership*
- Exercise 6.3: *Imagining the Positive*
- The *Imagining the Positive* visualization script or audio (the script can be found in chapter 6 of the client workbook and this therapist guide; the audio file can be accessed at the Treatments *That Work*™ website: www.oxfordclinicalpsych.com/PAT).

Goals

- Review content from last session and answer any questions.
- Educate the client on the role of attending to the positive.
- Introduce the skill of *Finding the Silver Linings*, facilitate a practice in session, and assign a practice for homework.
- Introduce the skill of *Taking Ownership*, facilitate a practice in session, and assign a practice for homework.
- Introduce the skill of *Imagining the Positive*, facilitate a practice in session, and assign a practice for homework.

Summary of Information in Chapter 6 of Client Workbook

- Individuals with anhedonia report difficulties in (a) noticing positive aspects of situations, (b) taking ownership over positive outcomes, and (c) imagining positive outcomes for events.
- The skill of *Finding the Silver Linings* helps to train attention toward positive aspects of situations.
- The skill of *Taking Ownership* helps individuals identify contributions they made toward positive outcomes.
- The skill of *Imagining the Positive* improves the ability to imagine possible positive outcomes.

■ These practices are introduced to improve positive emotions; they target liking, wanting, and learning.

Key Concepts

The key concept of this chapter is the introduction of new skills to shift attention toward positive stimuli, to recognize and reinforce positive behaviors the client engages in, and to improve prospective positive mental imagery. It is expected that you will use at least three sessions to introduce these skills—one session per practice. Goals for the client are to:

■ Improve the ability to notice positive stimuli in situations.
■ Improve the ability to recognize and take ownership over behaviors that have resulted in positive outcomes.
■ Increase the ability to imagine positive outcomes to events.

Importance of Attending to the Positive

The goal of this chapter is to learn to focus attention on positive experiences through repeated skills training. These skills address deficits in anticipation of reward by:

1. Having the client notice more of the positive (i.e., sustained attention to the positive), which helps to anticipate/prefer positive outcomes in the future (wanting)
2. Having the client appreciate (appraise stimuli more positively) and savor the positive, which increases the hedonic experience (liking)
3. Encouraging the client to learn to attribute their own actions to the positive (learning)

Instead of discounting negative appraisals (as is typical in cognitive restructuring), the primary goal of this chapter is to shift attention to positive features of situations. The underlying assumption is that mood will become more positive and positive stimuli will become preferred over negative stimuli, which in turn will encourage further attention to positive features of experiences. Together this will lead to more positive appraisals of situations. For example, the skill of *Taking Ownership* encourages clients to recognize ways in which their own behaviors have contributed to positive outcomes.

The reason for targeting attention is because evidence shows that depressed mood and anhedonia are associated with limited sustained attention to positive stimuli (i.e., noticing the positive). This is often observed clinically by a tendency to dismiss positive experiences and to devote attention and ruminative thinking disproportionately to negative experiences. This chapter explicitly targets sustained attention to positive features of past, present, and future experiences.

The focus on past and present experiences is achieved by re-evaluating situations that already occurred or are occurring, with effortful recall and identification of positive features of those events or situations even when they occurred alongside negative features. This skill, *Finding the Silver Linings*, is a direct extension of the work done with *Savoring the Moment* of positive activities, wherein again the focus is on positive features of those events.

Similarly, *Taking Ownership* involves re-examining past or current situations with positive outcomes, ranging from minor to major, to identify ways in which the clients themselves contributed to the positive outcomes.

The skill of *Imagining the Positive* is about events in the future, and imagining successful outcomes. Here the goal is to build up the capacity for prospective positive imagery, which is limited in persons with depression and anxiety. Importantly, positive imagery training is not to be confused with positive prophesizing; in other words, the goal is not to increase the likelihood of positive outcomes but rather to build the capacity to imagine their occurrence.

As the therapist, you will provide a general introduction to the chapter by asking clients about their difficulties in attending to the positive, and explaining what the effects can be on an individual with anhedonia. You will describe how some people tend to ignore positive events in their lives, either by not thinking about positive experiences in the past or by not imagining or anticipating positive events in the future. You will ask clients if they notice themselves doing this, and if so, how it makes them feel. Similarly, you can describe how some people have difficulty recognizing or appreciating positive events when they occur. Such individuals may frequently tell themselves that good things never happen to them, or when positive things do happen, such as receiving a compliment, the client dismisses these as not genuine or real. Again, you can ask your clients if they notice themselves doing this, and if so, how it makes them feel. Using the same description and client self-reflection question, you can describe how some people have no difficulty recognizing the occurrence of a positive event, but they do have difficulty appreciating it. For example, they might recognize that they are getting a job promotion, but they do not experience joy from it. Some people take less ownership of the positive, or fail to take credit for the good things that happen.

You can then discuss the impact of each of these types of biases on mood. This will provide the rationale for the "Attending to the Positive" skill set: recognizing positive events and experiences and taking ownership where possible.

Finding the Silver Linings

To introduce the skill of *Finding the Silver Linings*, you may ask clients about the popular phrase "every cloud has a silver lining" and what it means to them. This phrase means that there are positive aspects to almost any situation. However, depression, anxiety, and other negative emotional states lead people to ignore the positive and focus instead on the negative. Thus the goal of this skill is to shift attention to the positive *even when there are negative parts of an experience*. In other words, the goal is to look for the positive, big or small, in any situation. You may give clients a few examples to get the ball rolling: (1) an argument with a friend that has a good ending, (2) a performance review at work that includes some areas of weakness and also tips on how to improve, or (3) feeling anxious at a social event but staying rather than leaving the situation.

Emphasize that *Finding the Silver Linings* will have a positive impact on mood and the client's likelihood of attending more often to the positive in the future. Remind your client that it may seem ridiculous or overly optimistic to focus on silver linings. This is partly because any new skill can seem odd at first, but with practice it will become more familiar and even second nature. And as part of this chapter, remind your client that they will be purposefully searching for more silver linings than would be typically expected, in order to develop the skill of attending to the positive. The notion is that we have to practice any skill more intensely and more frequently at first in order to develop something that can be sustained in the long run—so the skill-building phase will push *Finding the Silver Linings* to the extreme.

You can begin the exercise by asking your client to identify silver linings for something as simple as brushing their teeth (e.g., my teeth are healthier, I'm less likely to get cavities, my breath doesn't smell, people will be more likely to spend time with me, I'll have to go to the dentist less often, I will save money on root canals, I had a nice taste in my mouth, and there won't be something in my teeth to be embarrassed by). Or, a more complex example could be used—say, the client's boss reviewed a document they had submitted. The document was covered in red corrections and an entire hour was spent going over potential revisions. What might be some positives about this event? The client now knows how to correct the document, and the boss spent a full hour of time giving corrective feedback to the employee. Now the client knows the boss's preferences, and now the boss knows that the employee can respond to criticisms. This may even improve their training.

If your client demonstrates a good understanding of the skill, ask them to choose an event that happened to them recently. This event should be one that was judged to be neutral or negative (although not traumatic; see later in the chapter). The client should then begin to generate positive features of this event using Exercise 6.1: Finding the Silver Linings, which can be found in the client workbook and also in the appendix at the end of this therapist guide). Clients may photocopy this exercise from the workbook or download multiple copies at the Treatments *That Work*™ website (www.oxfordclinicalpsych.com/PAT).

First, have the client rate their current mood state (on the 0-to-10 point mood scale with 0 for "lowest mood" and 10 for "highest mood"). Then work with the client to identify at least six positive features, being as creative as needed to generate the list. This can take some time, but is part of the learning process. Part of what this skill is attempting to address is the tendency to give up on identifying positive aspects when it's difficult to do so. After generating the silver linings, the client re-rates their mood and labels their positive emotions. By doing so, learning of reward is strengthened (i.e., the client learns that by expending effort to recognize positive aspects of past situations, they feel more positive emotions).

Remind your client that only after practice will the skills become easier, more automatic, and even more enjoyable; and, only after considerable practice will they see a long-term change in their mood. Should they indicate that although they did the exercise, they disliked it and did not notice an improvement in mood, validate this experience for them and inquire if they are attending to the meaning of what they are writing. For example, if a silver lining is "I am alive" or "I have shelter," what does that mean for them? By prompting more in-depth meaning, the exercise will be more effective. You may also ask them to compare it to how they would feel if these silver linings were not present.

Homework for Finding the Silver Linings

Clients may photocopy exercises from the workbook or download multiple copies at the Treatments *That Work*^{TM} website (www.oxfordclinicalpsych.com/PAT). For homework, ask your client to complete a *Finding the Silver Linings* practice each day. They can start with positive or neutral situations, which may be serious (e.g., visiting the doctor), silly (e.g., brushing their teeth), or meaningful (e.g., their child said, "mama"). But clients should eventually practice with more negative situations.

Case Vignette #1

In this vignette, the client is sharing the following types of thoughts in reaction to the *Finding the Silver Linings* practice: "What's the point of doing this? There was nothing positive in that situation."

C: *For homework, I tried to identify silver linings regarding an argument that I got into with my coworker last week, but I really don't understand the point of doing this. There was nothing positive in that situation.*

T: *I understand that the argument you had with your coworker was upsetting. I also know that practicing this skill of finding silver linings can be particularly hard to do when we are experiencing a negative mood state.*

C: *Yeah, I'm still really worked up about it. Talking about it now is making me feel pretty down, actually.*

T: *I can imagine. Being able to identify silver linings is a skill, one that develops the more we practice. We've talked about how our brains tend to be evolutionarily wired to pay attention to negative aspects of a situation, and so it is going to take dedicated practice to train our brains to also pay attention to positive aspects of a situation. When you find yourself feeling low and having a hard time identifying silver linings, it is an important signal that you likely need to continue or increase your practice.*

C: *I get that, I do. I know I tend to focus a lot on the negative, and I want to practice finding the positive. It is just hard to find the positive in something as unpleasant as an argument.*

T: *I agree that it is challenging to find silver linings with more negative situations, and it also creates a great opportunity to practice. I'm curious: Might we try to practice finding the silver lining with a different unpleasant activity? How about if we focus on something more neutral, something that we don't usually think of as having any positive aspects? What about an activity like brushing your teeth?*

C: *Well, sure. That's a pretty tedious activity, but I can try . . . I guess one positive thing I can think of is that brushing my teeth makes my breath smell better. It is also good for my long-term dental health.*

And hmm . . . I guess it also models good hygiene to my children? I'm always trying to get them to brush their teeth.

T: Those are all excellent silver linings! I think it's really interesting that you've taken such an everyday activity, like brushing your teeth, and have already identified several silver linings. Even though brushing your teeth is not necessarily pleasant or pleasurable in and of itself, you can identify positive or meaningful outcomes.

C: Yeah, it was nice to acknowledge those things. I guess I can see how similar silver linings might apply to my argument at work. For example, I know that it was important for me to air my grievances with my coworker, because I didn't want to suppress my feelings any longer; it was making me miserable at work.

T: I'm hearing that a silver lining was being able to get that upset off your chest and out into the open with your coworker.

C: Yes, and it was also important for me to speak up for myself. I don't always do that, and I can let things slide when people don't treat me nicely. It was good that I advocated for myself, even if it was unpleasant to do.

T: This is great work! Let's continue trying to identify a few more silver linings about this argument.

Case Vignette #2

The client's issue in this vignette is that by focusing on the positive, the client is concerned that the therapist is underestimating or not acknowledging the enormous challenges in the client's life.

C: I know you want me to find silver linings in my life, but it is really hard to focus on the positives right now. I have been feeling really isolated and it is difficult to get through the day being so disconnected from people during the pandemic. I feel like if I don't address my loneliness, it is going to get worse and I will feel even more depressed than I do right now.

T: I hear that; I know that your loneliness is causing you pain and that it has been very challenging to feel connected as of late. I don't want to discount how hard things have been for you recently or the importance of connection, but I do want us to take some time to revisit the nature of the work we are doing together so that we can be on the same page as to why we are particularly focused on positive thinking during this part of treatment.

C: Okay, I think that would be helpful because it feels like we are ignoring the challenges I'm facing, which really doesn't feel good.

T: In that case, I'm really glad we are setting aside some time to talk about this. One reason we are shifting the treatment focus to noticing the positive is that sometimes we find ourselves in situations where we can't change the outcome. For example, even though you started adding some social activities during the first part of treatment, you were limited by what you could do because of the pandemic. Given this reality, it's important to recognize what positive already exists, which will give you a change in perspective and then likely a change in how you feel. Not all of these skills can "fix" the difficult challenges you may be facing in your life. Instead, we view some of these skills as being of use as they can help you to better navigate negative emotions and difficult experiences when they inevitably occur.

C: That makes sense; I guess we don't expect silver linings to make the difficult things I'm going through disappear, but rather help me to cope with those challenges.

T: Absolutely. In fact, Finding the Silver Linings may help you recognize that you have more social connection than you previously realized, which may decrease some of those feelings of loneliness. That all being said, it is important to acknowledge the difficult experiences you've been having that have enormously contributed to your low mood. And, what you just highlighted is also true. The silver linings skill is meant to help you identify even just a few positive aspects of the situation you are facing—not to ignore or minimize the negative aspects, but to hopefully bring about more positive thinking, which in turn can lead to more positive emotions and mood.

C: That's helpful; I get it.

T: Great. I also want to acknowledge that practicing the silver linings skill is also helpful to us in the long term. Our brains often get used to identifying and focusing on negative aspects of a situation, and it takes a lot of practice to train our brains to increasingly identify and focus on positive aspects of a given situation as well. Positive thinking is like a muscle that we want to strengthen over time, and the only way to do that is through repeated, intentional practice. The more *we can train our brains to attend to the positive, the more balanced thinking we can expect to have in the future when we experience challenging circumstances.*

C: *I need to remember this—that even if positive thinking is awkward or difficult now, it will pay off in the future and eventually feel more natural.*

Case Vignette #3

In this vignette, the client views how well they avoided a situation as an example of a silver lining, whereas the therapist views the avoidance as maladaptive.

T: *Alright, let's practice applying silver linings to a somewhat challenging or negative experience from the past week.*

C: *Okay, I think we can try with my friend's Zoom birthday party I attended. My social anxiety really increased leading up to the party and got pretty bad during as well.*

T: *Okay. Taking stock of this Zoom birthday party, can you identify any silver linings? Any positive aspects of the situation you found yourself in?*

C: *Well, my anxiety decreased during the party. I showed up fashionably late so that I wouldn't have to deal with the awkward small talk at the beginning. I also kept myself on mute for most of the party and didn't say much. So I guess we can say a silver lining is that I found a way to keep my anxiety low?*

T: *I hear that keeping yourself on mute and showing up fashionably late are both things that were helpful in the short term—they reduced your anxiety in the moment—but with this skill it can actually be more helpful to focus on the silver linings that took place despite the fact that you experienced discomfort or anxiety.*

C: *So you want me to focus on my anxiety?*

T: *Not quite. I'm curious if we can instead focus on positive aspects of the situation that arose even though you experienced anxiety leading up to this event and during the event. This skill is about training our brains to identify positive aspects of the situation that we may typically overlook or fail to recognize. For example, it sounds like a silver lining was that you ended up going in the first place! You mentioned feeling anxious before, and even though you showed up late, you eventually attended the party. Does that feel like a silver lining from your perspective?*

C: Yeah, I guess the fact that I showed up at all is a positive for sure. I have been known to "flake" and skip events altogether. It definitely is a silver lining that I mustered up the confidence to attend.

T: *That's great. Are there any other silver linings that you can think of?*

C: I see. . . . Well, a second silver lining is that I kept my promise to my friend. I RSVP'd yes to the Zoom party and I followed through. I know it meant a lot to my friend that I showed up, even though I didn't say much on the call.

T: *Absolutely. These are great. I'm curious if there are any silver linings from the situation that are positive because of what you learned from the experience? Or things about your experience that will be helpful to you moving forward?*

C: Let me think . . . You know, I guess I learned that even if I am feeling anxious, I can get through the whole party without needing to leave early. Sure, I kept myself on mute and didn't speak up much, but I got through it. The anxiety didn't kill me. I feel like I can be more confident going to my next Zoom gathering.

T: *I think that's great. I am actually hearing two silver linings: You learned from this experience that you can get through it, and next time you will feel more confident to attend.*

C: You're right! There are quite a few silver linings to unpack there.

Troubleshooting for Finding the Silver Linings

One of the most common issues that arise from the practice of *Finding the Silver Linings* is perception of invalidation, because from the client's perspective, this skill does not address the "real" issues they are facing. Clients are typically seeking help at the point of peak distress, with a strong desire to focus on the negative emotional experiences and environmental events, to either understand them or fix them. The goal of the Positive Affect Treatment (PAT) therapist is to balance validation of the client's distress and undesirable life circumstances with the value of improving mood through attending to the positive; by attending to the positive, the occurrence or impact of negative emotions or negative events will be lessened, and the client will be in a better "emotional place" to more effectively manage their negative emotions or negative events. It is also an opportunity for you to reinforce the notion that the pull of negativity is the very thing that is being targeted by this treatment strategy—for the client to learn to shift away from negativity and toward positivity.

You can inform clients that there may be occasions of frustration because you will continually refocus their attention onto the positive even though the client is drawn to discuss negative experiences. Being overly drawn to the negative is the very thing that is being targeted by this treatment, so you can validate the pull of negative events, the negative impact of staying on the negative, and the value of emotion regulation through shifting attention. In essence, you will reassure the client that negative emotions and negative events are significant in their lives, and that directly targeting the negativity is not the only (nor the best) way to find relief; instead, this treatment builds positive capacity so that negative emotions and events fade in significance or become more manageable.

You can validate that it might feel strange, unfamiliar, or even risky to ignore the negative experiences, but nonetheless encourage clients to experiment with evaluating the power of refocusing their attention on the positive, even in the midst of negative events. The benefit from attending to the positive will depend on how much clients lean into these skills, since the pull to focus on the negative may continually tug them away. In these cases, the notion of training can be helpful—training to build up the muscle of positivity to be stronger than the muscle of negativity. There may be occasions when, even though the client has agreed to the therapeutic rationale, they continue to focus on the negative. You can validate the client and then remind them of the treatment rationale.

Sometimes clients indicate that they cannot think of even one positive feature of a situation. In this case, you can validate the difficulty of generating positive features particularly when we are in a negative mood state, and then restate the skill-building aspect of this treatment, and the very fact that the difficulty identifying positive features indicates that this approach is the right one. Then, start with a silly or mundane practice such as identifying positive features of brushing one's teeth, cutting finger nails, or yawning.

There will be some events in the client's history for which the skill of *Finding the Silver Linings* is not appropriate—specifically, traumatic events. Talking about trauma can trigger appropriately intense emotions and is beyond the scope of this particular attention skill. While some people can find meaning and growth following trauma, that typically involves more extensive work with trauma-focused treatments. Hence, we do not encourage applying *Finding the Silver Linings* to traumatic experiences, at least not in the absence of prior prolonged exposure or cognitive processing therapy around the trauma.

Another concern that can arise is when clients escape a situation due to panic, anxiety, or overwhelming distress. In these cases, steer the client away from considering avoidance as a positive and attempt to identify other positive features of the situation (e.g., the client entered the situation even though anxious, learned what to do differently next time).

Finally, some clients may report that they have no problem attending to the positive. In those cases, it is possible to skip this chapter, but we generally recommend continuing with the chapter regardless, since clients may discover biases toward the negative or room for improvement as they proceed.

Taking Ownership

The next skill in this chapter, *Taking Ownership*, teaches the client to take credit for ways in which they contribute to positive outcomes. This skill specifically targets reward learning, or realizing that by one's own actions, rewards can be achieved. Taking credit where due is a relevant skill since depression and anhedonia are associated with a biased attributional style, whereby negative outcomes are attributed to oneself and positive outcomes are attributed to others or other circumstances. Diminishing self-attribution for positive outcomes not only limits the learning of reward (i.e., "if I do this behavior, I will be likely to get that positive outcome") but also reduces the motivation to engage in behaviors likely to lead to reward in the future.

Begin this section by informing your client that it is common for people to have difficulties seeing how their behavior produces good things for them. For example, if a situation or event goes well, an individual might attribute the positive outcome to luck rather than to their own contribution. Ask your client if this resonates with them. Then discuss the impact of this attributional bias—specifically, that failing to recognize how our behavior contributes to a positive event decreases the likelihood that we will engage in the same behaviors in the future, even though the behaviors make events more positive. This is because our memory of events and past behavior becomes a blueprint for future events. Knowing how our behavior contributed to a positive event will reinforce that behavior and lead to more positive events in the future. Moreover, it will contribute to the anticipation and motivation to do other behaviors that may lead to positive outcomes. That is because the sense of control engendered by knowing that we can contribute to the likelihood of a positive outcome motivates behavior in that direction. *Taking Ownership* of positive events occurring in our lives is just as important as noticing that these positive events exist. Before we can create positive events in our lives, we first must believe that we can affect and influence certain positive things.

You can then lead a practice with the client by identifying a positive event that has occurred in the relatively recent past (e.g., showing up for therapy, having an enjoyable time with a friend, volunteering) and asking the client to identify and highlight what their contributions were to the event, using Exercise 6.2: Taking Ownership, which can be found in the client workbook and also in the appendix at the end of this therapist guide. Completing this exercise may take time, but it is important to persist, be creative, and identify even the most minor ways in which the client may have contributed to an outcome. Next, it can be helpful to have the client to "sit with" (or reflect upon and appreciate) *Taking Ownership* of the positive outcomes. This can be done by writing out and then verbally stating out loud what their contributions were as they look in the mirror. The goal here is to deepen the client's experience of reward. You may encourage your client to show positive body movements (e.g., smile) as they verbally state out loud their own contributions. After reading out loud, they can then sit quietly and reflect on their contribution. Next, ask your client to re-rate their mood and label their emotional response to deepen the emotional experience and learn reward (i.e., "by reflecting on my contributions to positive events, my mood is more positive").

Homework for Taking Ownership

Clients may photocopy exercises from the workbook or download multiple copies at the Treatments *That Work*™ website (www.oxfordclinicalpsych.com/PAT). For homework, ask your client to complete one *Taking Ownership* exercise each day.

Case Vignettes for Taking Ownership

Case Vignette #1

The client's issue is that they don't feel as if they deserve any credit for a positive outcome because they are not worthy.

T: *Let's practice identifying how you contributed to a positive event that occurred in the past week. Is there something good that happened that you can think of as an example?*

C: *I had a nice dinner with my family last night, but I don't really see how I had anything to do with that.*

T: *Tell me about that.*

C: *As I mentioned, I've been feeling pretty down on myself lately because I've hardly been able to keep up with work and taking care of the kids. If anything, I feel like it's my fault that things go wrong all the time and my house is a mess.*

T: *Yes, you certainly have a lot on your plate right now. Do you often find yourself taking all the blame when things go wrong?*

C: *All the time. I feel like I can't do anything right.*

T: *And what about when something goes well? Do you "blame" yourself for positive things, too?*

C: *No, of course not. I don't deserve the credit.*

T: *It's common for people to take all of the ownership for bad things and none for good things. If you think about it, it's really quite unfair! The purpose of this skill is to balance out that tendency by training our brains to notice when we contribute to positive events in our lives. It may feel challenging at first, but with practice it will become easier and can help improve the way you feel about yourself.*

C: *When you put it that way, I guess it is lopsided for me to do that to myself. I can't help but feel pretty worthless, though.*

T: *Would you be willing to give it a try? Let's return to the nice dinner you had last night. What did you do that led to having dinner? For example, did you make these plans?*

C: *Well, I have to put dinner on the table every night for my kids. So yes, I made pasta for them.*

T: *Great! So one major contribution is that you cooked the meal. What were all of the steps that went into that? Did the water boil itself?*

C: *I guess you're right: I did have to think ahead by going grocery shopping, assembling the ingredients for my kids' favorite pasta sauce, and making a salad.*

T: *Wow, I heard you just come up with three more things you did to contribute to the dinner. Another part of what I'm hearing is that you were quite thoughtful and even anticipated what your kids would like to eat. Do you think that being a caring mother and listening to your kids' preferences in the past contributed to the nice dinner, too? Let's see if we can come up with a few more things to add- and really build this muscle.*

C: *Yeah, I guess I'm a better mom than I give myself credit for. I also invited over my sister because I know the kids always love seeing her. We were all laughing together. I'm surprised I was able to come up with a few things. In my mind it was just another night, but breaking it down like this helps me see all the little things that I did to make it happen.*

T: *You're exactly right. It is very easy to discount these experiences by glossing over them. But it seems like your efforts positively impacted your family members, who I know you really care about.*

Case Vignette #2

In this vignette, the client is not comfortable accepting ownership and fears being judged for doing so.

C: I don't like talking about the things I did well. Won't getting too good at this skill make me arrogant?

T: I hear your concern and want to understand more. Where did you learn that taking ownership for your contributions would mean you are arrogant?

C: I guess it's always been a part of my family values. My parents taught me that no one is better than anyone else and it's conceited to brag about your accomplishments. If they saw me talking this way they'd probably call me on it.

T: I think it is important to distinguish between excessively bragging to other people versus noticing for yourself what you contributed to positive events, which is the focus of this skill. Do you see a difference there?

C: It makes sense that it doesn't necessarily mean rubbing it in other people's faces or comparing to other people. But why would it be helpful to notice what I do well for just myself?

T: Good question! A lot of people with low mood tend to ignore their role when good things happen, which can lower their mood even further and contribute to a sense of powerlessness. Further, not taking responsibility for the positive things in our lives reduces the likelihood of positive events happening in the future. Why do you think that might be?

C: I'm not sure. When good things happen, I feel like it was random or I just got lucky. Maybe realizing my contribution could help me feel more in control?

T: Exactly! Disregarding our contributions can decrease the chances of positive things happening again because we never learn how to generate them. On the flip side, recognizing our contributions can help us do more of what was effective, in order to increase the chances that positive outcomes will happen in the future.

C: Okay, I get it now and can give it a try even though it feels weird.

T: Great! Like all new skills in this treatment or in life, it might feel uncomfortable at first but will become easier with practice. Let's think through this with an example.

Case Vignette #3

In this situation, the client fears that feeling positive emotions about their contributions will lead to complacency. They do not allow themselves to feel positively due to a belief about what they "should" be doing as their duty.

C: *If I pat myself on the back all the time, won't I become complacent? I'm afraid I'll become even less motivated to do schoolwork because anxiety is one of the only things that drives me.*

T: *I know you've talked about how important your academic goals are to you, like getting good grades and graduating from college. It sounds like anxiety, along with a fear of failure and self-critical thoughts, can be a motivator in the short term. However, how does being driven by worry affect your energy and motivation in the long term?*

C: *I'm drained all the time and after the adrenaline rush ends, I crash. But I'm afraid to be too relaxed or too positive.*

T: *Would you be willing to try out the skill this week? We can treat it like an experiment to test out whether taking ownership of your contributions does indeed affect your motivation. In fact, positive emotions—such as feeling accomplished, proud, and excited—can often energize us to do more, especially in the future.*

C: *I'm willing to try it. I just don't like the idea of feeling good about myself for things I should be doing anyway. Because my parents are paying for college, being a good student is my duty. I don't have the right to feel proud of myself.*

T: *I'm glad you shared that with me; "should" thoughts can cause us to be really hard on ourselves. Let's imagine one of your friends from college. Do you judge them for feeling proud of themselves after they do well on an exam?*

C: *No. I feel happy for them and want my friends to feel good.*

T: *I'm hearing that when someone shares their accomplishments with you, you even feel positive emotions too! Why do you think it might be helpful for your friends to feel proud of themselves for studying in order to do well on an exam?*

C: *Because it's like positive reinforcement, right? Then my friends would be rewarded and might feel more motivated to study in the future.*

T: Exactly! What would it be like to apply this same logic to yourself? Let's try out an example by identifying your contributions to a positive event that happened this week.

C: I did really well on my biology midterm earlier this week. I made flashcards to help me study. I got a 90%—but I can't help but dwell on the 10% I got wrong.

T: Great job identifying that you put in the effort to make flashcards! I'm also impressed that you're noticing the natural tendency for our minds to drift to the negative. I'm not suggesting that you should ignore your mistakes or room for improvement. Instead, I wonder whether it could be equally important to really understand what you did that contributed to the 90% you got right. This skill of Taking Ownership trains our brains to also focus on our own positive behavior.

C: That makes me feel better that I don't have to ignore what I got wrong, but that it's more about balancing out what I focus on.

Troubleshooting for Taking Ownership

For some clients, identifying the positive event may be the hardest part. Validate this, and emphasize that identifying positive events in one's life is another important skill to practice. For clients who report that they do not have any positive experiences in their lives, you may include their activities that were completed as part of their Positive Activity Scheduling (Exercise 5.5). Or, you may also ask the client what behaviors they had to do in order to come to the session today.

The natural tendency of anhedonia and depressed mood is to dismiss positivity, including the ways in which one may have contributed to positive outcomes. Encourage clients to lean into the reflection of ownership—to deeply reflect upon how their own actions contributed to certain positive outcomes.

Occasionally, fear of expressing positive contributions may emerge when clients worry about being judged negatively by others for assuming a role they don't feel they deserve. They may worry that they are irresponsibly ignoring negative emotions or negative events. Again, balance validation of those feelings with the fact that they represent the pull of negativity, and the value of learning to weaken that pull is by focusing instead on positive elements.

Clients' doubts about this skill may emerge in comments that it has only a limited value in the larger picture of their negative life experiences (i.e., "How does accepting my small contributions matter when I have so much going wrong in my life?"). Here, you can validate these concerns, but re-emphasize that building positive capacity will enable the client to be less overwhelmed and more able to cope with negative parts of life.

Imagining the Positive

The last skill covered in this chapter is *Imagining the Positive*, which targets the anticipation and motivation for reward as well as savoring the attainment of reward, with secondary effects upon learning of reward by having clients rate their mood before and after each exercise. This set of exercises targets the impoverished positive mental imagery (Holmes et al., 2016) and bias to interpret ambiguous information negatively (Rude et al., 2002) that characterize depression and anhedonia.

Introduce this topic by exploring whether clients have difficulty envisioning or anticipating future events going well for them and instead assume that future events will go poorly. You can then explore the consequences of anticipating negative outcomes. Imagination can be a blueprint for future behavior. Imagining a situation going well can teach and prepare an individual to respond in a way that enhances the likelihood of that event going well (although this skill will not guarantee positive outcomes and should not be confused with simple prophesizing). Since the evidence suggests that mood is more likely to be boosted with greater vividness of the visualization, encourage clients to use all of their senses in this skill (sight, hearing, smell, taste, and touch/temperature).

Ask your client to identify an event that is expected to occur in the next week. Examples might include going to the next treatment appointment, meeting a friend, or presenting at work. Using Exercise 6.3: Imagining the Positive, which can be found in the client workbook and also in the appendix at the end of this therapist guide, clients write about the situation going well for them prior to starting the visualization as an aid. Some clients find it difficult to begin a visualization without writing out the future event more positively first.

Then engage your client in a visualization, which has similarities to *Savoring the Moment*. Using the following steps, guide your client through a visualization of their future situation going well, with the client sharing out loud the events in present tense:

- Remind them to use all of their senses and that they should envision the situation positively.
- Inform them that they might notice a tendency or urge to imagine the situation negatively, but request that they do their best to push themselves toward the positive.
- Have them think of a starting point for themselves (e.g., a few minutes before the event or when the event starts).
- Have them walk slowly through the future event, in present tense as it unfolds in front of their eyes.
- Stop frequently to encourage your client to describe thoughts, emotions, and physical sensations they are experiencing.
- Ask them to rate their mood on the exercise form before and after the visualization.

After the visualization, guide the client to process how they felt imagining the situation and reinforce changes in their mood as a result of the visualization. Reinforce labeling of a variety of positive emotions such as joy, excitement, curiosity, and happiness. If your client has difficulty identifying positive emotions, encourage them to describe how it feels in their body to have a particular emotion (e.g., feeling lighter or warmer) or use labels from Exercise 6.3: Imagining the Positive.

Box 6.1 provides an example of a visualization script for *Imagining the Positive* that can be used for homework; note that a 🌐 recording of this script is available for both your clients and you on the Treatments *That Work™* website (www.oxfordclinicalpsych.com/PAT).

Homework for Imagining the Positive

Clients may photocopy exercises from the workbook or download multiple copies at the Treatments *That Work™* website (www.oxfordclinicalpsych.com/PAT). For homework, ask your clients to complete a visualization of a positive future event each day over the

Box 6.1 Visualization Script for Imagining the Positive

Gently get yourself into a comfortable position with your feet flat on the ground, your back upright but not too stiff, and hands in your lap. If you feel comfortable, gently close your eyes or rest them on a spot in front of you. Bring to mind an image of your surroundings at your starting point.

Imagine where you are as vividly as possible. Notice what you see around you . . . smells . . . sounds . . . temperature. Do you notice a nice aroma? Do you notice sounds of nature or other noises? Is it warm or cool? Do you feel a nice breeze? Take a moment to notice your surroundings. (Pause)

Now shift your attention to your own body in that future moment. What are the physical symptoms you are feeling? Are you feeling a rush of adrenaline? A release of tension? Perhaps a positive racing of the heart or a smile on your face? (Pause)

What are the emotions you are feeling? Excitement? Peace? Joy? Curiosity? Compassion? Interest? Imagine feeling one of these positive feelings and what it might feel like in your body. (Pause)

Now identify your thoughts in this future context. How can you make them more positive? (Pause)

Begin to slowly walk yourself through the events that you wrote down on your exercise form. Take time to notice your positive thoughts, emotions, and bodily sensations as you walk yourself through those positive events. (Pause)

Notice what your future self would be feeling now . . . thinking now . . . (Allow minutes to pass)

Whenever you are ready, gently bring your attention back to the room, and open your eyes.

next week, with each practice lasting at least five minutes. Clients can practice by listening to the audio, reading the script, imagining without using any aid, or recording and listening to themselves read the script.

Case Vignettes for Imagining the Positive

Case Vignette #1

This vignette is an example of how to encourage clients to imagine positive future events if they do not believe positive things will happen.

T: *Let's try to imagine a positive event that could happen in the future.*

C: *I don't think that this is going to be helpful for me.*

T: *Tell me more about that.*

C: I don't think anything positive is going to happen to me in the future. Things have felt so hard for so long, and I don't really experience anything positive in my day-to-day life. Why would I imagine something I don't think is going to happen? More than that, why would imagining something even help me?

T: It can be hard to imagine positive things happening in the future when you've been experiencing a low mood for so long. As we've discussed previously, mood and thoughts are connected, and when people are in a low mood, it is much harder to think about positive things that may happen in life. That being said, we have found that by attending to the positive, mood becomes more positive.

C: Okay.

T: Attending to the positive is like strengthening a muscle. How do you gain strength?

C: Training or practice?

T: Exactly. Imagining the positive is a way to give your brain practice in attending to the positive. The more you imagine the positive, the more we expect that you will notice improvements in your mood. Would you be willing to brainstorm some positive things that might happen in the future?

C: I guess, but like I said, I really can't think of anything.

T: I wonder if it might be helpful to turn back to the positive activity list we made at the start of treatment.

C: Okay.

T: Looking at that list, are there any positive events you wrote down that you could imagine happening in the future?

C: Well, I wrote down "spend time with my daughter." She lives far away, and I don't see her often, so I'm not sure it would ever happen.

T: Great work identifying a positive event. It sounds like seeing your daughter, or going on a trip to visit her, could be a positive and very meaningful experience for you. This skill is all about imagining a positive thing that could happen, so it's okay if you aren't sure if it would happen. Are you willing to walk through this event with me as if it were playing out in real time?

C: Yes, I can try it.

Case Vignette #2

This vignette is an example of how to encourage clients to imagine positive future events if they have other major life stressors.

T: Today I want to talk through a new skill that we call *Imagining the Positive*.

C: Okay.

T: *Imagining the Positive* is another form of attending to the positive. We generally find that when people are able to imagine positive things happening in the future, their mood becomes more positive.

C: It feels kind of like you're telling me that simply thinking about positive things happening in the future is going to make everything better. That seems a little short-sighted to me. . . . I have so many real problems in my life; in what world is *Imagining the Positive* going to improve the fact that I am chronically ill, working full time to try to make ends meet and take care of my kids, and feeling like I don't have any friends or family to support me right now?

T: I hear you. And you know what? You're right. You are juggling so much right now. *Imagining the Positive* isn't going to fix all of those real problems. But *Imagining the Positive* is one skill that we can add to your toolbox. The overarching goal here is to find ways to appreciate and experience positive events more deeply. Can you think of any ways that *Imagining the Positive* might be beneficial to your life?

C: I guess I'm often focused on which bad thing is going to happen, so if I wasn't thinking about that all of the time, maybe I'd feel better.

T: I think that's a great point. It sounds like you've experienced the ways that anticipating the negative might actually make you feel worse. So, it's possible that focusing on the positive could make you feel better!

C: Yes, I guess it could help in some ways.

T: What do you think life might look like for you if you were able to more automatically appreciate and experience the positive?

C: I mean, I'd like to think that maybe if I was expecting good things to happen, I'd be doing more in general. Maybe I'd try to see friends or do new activities.

T: I've heard you say now that maybe life might look a little different if you were able to more automatically think about, anticipate, and savor the positive. Again, I'm not saying that this skill will take away all of the challenging things in your life. However, I'm wondering *if, given that this has the chance to boost your mood, you might be willing to give this skill a try?*

C: *Yes, I'm open to trying it.*

Case Vignette #3

This vignette demonstrates the process of using Imagining the Positive with clients who state that the skill makes them feel worse.

T: *Let's imagine a positive event that could happen in the future. I'd like you to walk me through this event in present tense, describing any emotions and physical sensations that arise in the moment. This is similar to what we did in our first sessions, but instead of recounting something you've already done, we will focus on something positive that could happen in the future. Do you have an idea of an event we could use for this exercise?*

C: *Yes. I really used to like traveling and I have always wanted to go to Paris with my daughter and show her the Notre Dame.*

T: *Great! Why don't you start by telling me what you see when you imagine being in Paris with your daughter, looking at the Notre Dame?*

C: *Well, I am excited to finally be here with her. I am holding my daughter's hand while I point to the gargoyles on the building's exterior. My daughter thinks they look funny and laughs. I walk with my daughter around the perimeter of the building and tell her about the big fire that happened. I'm starting to feel melancholy in this moment. I had been to Paris years ago when I studied abroad. I was so full of energy and joy and adventurousness. Now, I feel like I've lost that spark. I feel like the world I'm showing my daughter is darker and sadder.* (Client becomes tearful.)

T: *It makes perfect sense to feel saddened by the ways life and the world has changed since you first saw the Notre Dame when you were younger. I do want to take a moment to notice the ways your mind is being pulled to the negative in this situation. I am wondering if you might be able to return to this moment with your daughter and continue to imagine the positive emotions and sensations that could arise in this situation?*

C: *I'm sorry, but I just don't know if I can keep doing this. I know this is supposed to make me feel better, but I just feel worse after realizing how off course I am from where I hoped to be.*

T: *I hear that this has been a painful exercise for you. I want to remind you that this is a skill to learn and practice. It can feel very challenging at first. However, the only way to get better at something like this is to keep practicing. We've talked in the past about how doing these exercises is similar to weight training. Continued practice with the skill will strengthen your brain's ability to imagine the positive and to savor that experience. Do you think your mood could look different if you were able to imagine the positive more easily?*

C: *I guess it might. Maybe I'd just be less pessimistic overall. I wouldn't always be expecting the worst scenario. Is it possible that thinking good things might happen could lead to more positivity? I'm not really sure . . .*

T: *I think you're exactly right. We often find that when people are able to use this skill, they are more motivated to engage in activities that produce positive outcomes. When positive outcomes do occur, practicing these skills often enables people to really savor the positive aspects of experiences more thoroughly, which tends to increase positive emotions.*

C: *That makes sense.*

T: *I'm wondering if now, after reminding yourself why this activity could help, you might be willing to return to our exercise and try to keep your attention focused on the positive?*

C: *Yes, it might be hard, but I think I can do that.*

T: *Wonderful. So, you're outside of the Notre Dame with your daughter . . .*

Troubleshooting for Imagining the Positive

For clients who report difficulty identifying positive future events, they can choose a past activity from Positive Activity Scheduling (Exercise 5.5) and imagine that it's an upcoming future activity.

Some clients may find this skill invalidating, given their dire life circumstances. In this case, validate their life circumstances, and at the same time remind them that the goal of this chapter is not to change their life conditions but to rebalance mood in a more positive direction, and that by so doing, life circumstances will be more effectively managed.

Finally, some clients may find the exercise induces negative emotions and rumination since the contrast reminds them of what they do not have. In this case, you can again validate, and at the same time, remind clients that the skill of being able to imagine positive future events is designed to build the muscle for positivity. This skill will eventually lead clients to be more motivated to engage in behaviors that will be more likely to lead to positive outcomes and to savor such outcomes when they do occur, which will in turn contribute to positive emotions and lessen negative emotions.

CHAPTER 7 Building Positivity

(Corresponds to chapter 7 of client workbook)

Materials Needed

- Electronic device to play audio (optional)
- Exercise 7.1: Loving-Kindness (all exercises are included in the client workbook and also included in the appendix at the end of this therapist guide)
- The guided instructions for practicing Loving-Kindness script or audio (the script can be found in chapter 7 of the client workbook and this therapist guide; the audio file can be accessed at the Treatments *That Work*™ website: www.oxfordclinicalpsych.com/PAT).
- Exercise 7.2: Gratitude
- Exercise 7.3: Generosity
- Exercise 7.4: Appreciative Joy
- The guided instructions for practicing Appreciative Joy script or audio (the script can be found in chapter 7 of the client workbook and this therapist guide; the audio file can be accessed at the Treatments *That Work*™ website: www.oxfordclinicalpsych.com/PAT).

Goals

- Review content from last session and answer any questions.
- Explain the science that supports the four positive practices introduced in this chapter.
- Introduce *Loving-Kindness*, lead a practice in *Loving-Kindness*, and assign *Loving-Kindness* practice for homework.
- Introduce the benefits of *Gratitude*, lead a *Gratitude* exercise, and assign *Gratitude* homework.
- Introduce the benefits of *Generosity* and assign *Generosity* homework.
- Introduce *Appreciative Joy*, lead a practice in *Appreciative Joy*, and assign *Appreciative Joy* practice for homework.
- Review key concepts from this chapter.

- *Loving-Kindness* is a practice, where one visualizes a living being or the world, to which loving and kind thoughts are offered. It has been shown to improve one's mental health and well-being, as well as feelings of connectedness.
- *Gratitude* is an emotion, behavior, and thought strategy. When used regularly as a skill, it has been shown to result in many positive mental health benefits.
- *Generosity* is the act of giving by choice, and it is limitless if defined creatively. Regularly practicing *Generosity* can result in increased happiness and can reduce the effect of negative outcomes on mood.
- *Appreciative Joy* is the experience of positive emotions that emerge from the success of others. It is also the practice of offering positive thoughts of continued good fortune to another. It can improve positive affect, like the other positive practices.

Key Concepts

The key concepts of this chapter are building positivity through four new skills that have been practiced for centuries and demonstrated by research to increase positive emotions. We expect that you will use at least four sessions to introduce these skills—one session per skill. Clients will learn how to practice *Loving-Kindness* and *Appreciative Joy* to generate feelings of love, joy, and connection. They will also learn how to apply the skills of *Generosity* and *Gratitude* to their daily lives. Goals for the client are to:

- Begin a practice of *Loving-Kindness*.
- Incorporate daily acts of *Gratitude*.
- Build acts of *Generosity* into their week.
- Experiment with a practice of *Appreciative Joy*.

In this chapter, you will introduce four skills: *Loving-Kindness*, *Gratitude*, *Generosity*, and *Appreciative Joy*. What is key to emphasize here is that centuries of cultural practice and an abundance of research demonstrate the positive effects of these skills or practices on one's mental health, well-being, and relationships (Algoe & Haidt, 2009; DeShea, 2003; Emmons & McCullough, 2003; McCullough et al., 2002; Van Overwalle et al., 1995; Wood et al., 2008b). Unfortunately, these skills are often misunderstood because of their vague or multiple descriptions. Therefore, describing and practicing these skills in session with the client will be essential. This applies even to *Gratitude* and *Generosity*, which are universal human experiences.

It is important for you to review the science and history behind each of these concepts with your clients. This can be done by dedicating a separate session to each positive practice, which is the recommended option. Each session begins with a review of homework from the prior session, followed by an introduction of the science and history of the next "Building Positivity" skills. Then you will lead a practice of the exercise, followed by a discussion of the client's experience. At the end of session, there is another review of the session's content and assigning of homework. Another option is to review all of the science and history of these skills in a single session before dedicating additional sessions to the practice of these exercises.

The order of how to introduce these positive practices is up to you as the therapist; however, as indicated in the workbook, we recommend the following order: *Loving-Kindness*, *Gratitude*, *Generosity*, and *Appreciative Joy*. There are multiple reasons for this. It can be beneficial to start with the skill of *Loving-Kindness*, which sometimes requires extra time and practice for its benefits to surface. Also, a feeling of *Gratitude* (the next recommended skill) is often cultivated during this practice. Research has shown that *Gratitude* predicts prosocial behavior, like *Generosity* (Emmons & McCullough, 2003), which is the next skill we suggest covering. Finally, acts of *Generosity* provide fantastic situations with which to practice *Appreciative Joy*— the final skill.

Background

Loving-Kindness began as an Eastern spiritual practice and has been gaining more prominence in the West as a secular practice. It involves focusing one's awareness on loving and kind concern for other living beings, oneself, and the world (Hofmann et al., 2011). It has also been described as an act of training one's emotional experience toward warmth and tenderness, using an open orientation (Garland et al., 2010). During a practice, one visualizes a living being or the world, to which loving and kind thoughts are offered. There is a mindful awareness of thoughts, emotions, and sensations that arise.

Loving-Kindness interventions have been shown to increase positive affect (Fredrickson et al., 2008; Hutcherson et al., 2008; Zeng et al., 2015) and decrease negative affect (Hutcherson et al., 2008), including anger, pain, and distress (Carson et al., 2005). Some research suggests that *Loving-Kindness* meditation reduces anhedonia as a negative symptom of schizophrenia (Johnson et al., 2009). This practice has also been shown to increase feelings of connection to others (Hutcherson et al., 2008).

In PAT, we use *Loving-Kindness* to target reward attainment, or liking. Through a *Loving-Kindness* practice, one notices and appreciates loving and kind emotions, thoughts, and physical symptoms. Koole and colleagues (1999) demonstrated that self-affirmations following failure led to less rumination and increased positive affect, suggesting that *Loving-Kindness* toward oneself may lead to changes in negative thinking, which results in increased positive affect. Further, Fredrickson and colleagues (2008) found that increases in positive emotions following *Loving-Kindness* predicted change in resources, which was associated with change in life satisfaction.

How to Practice Loving-Kindness

You will lead the client through a *Loving-Kindness* exercise in session by reading the guided instructions script in Box 7.1 or playing the audio.

Ensure that the client records their mood beforehand using the Exercise 7.1: Loving-Kindness form, which can be found in the client workbook and also in the appendix at the end of this therapist guide. A ⬤ recording of the script is available for both you and your clients on the Treatments *That Work*™ website (www.oxfordclinicalpsych.com/PAT), and clients may photocopy this exercise from the workbook or download multiple copies from the website.

Box 7.1 Guided Instructions for Practicing Loving-Kindness

Find a comfortable position someplace with little to no distractions. It can be helpful to sit in a chair with your feet flat on the ground, your back upright, and your eyes closed or gently resting on a spot in front of you.

If you notice that your mind is racing, wandering, or being especially distractible today, take a moment to gently shift your attention to your breath, by noticing each inhalation and each exhalation. Observe the changes in your body as you take air in and as you release it. Notice your belly rising and falling or the change in temperature of the air traveling in and out of your nose.

Whenever you are ready, begin by identifying someone who you like and who is uncomplicated. This can be someone who you deeply care about, even a pet, or it can be someone who you know from a distance but greatly respect. Imagine them sitting in front of you, smiling, and looking back at you.

Offer them the following statements, focusing on the words as you say them aloud or in your mind:

> *I wish you peace . . .*
>
> *I wish you health . . .*
>
> *I hope you are without distress, hardship, or misfortune . . .*
>
> *I wish you love and joy . . .*
>
> *. . .*
>
> *I wish you peace . . .*
>
> *I wish you health . . .*
>
> *I hope you are without distress, hardship, or misfortune . . .*
>
> *I wish you love and joy . . .*

(continued)

Box 7.1 Continued

Notice what emotions and physical sensations emerge as you offer these statements. Warmth? A smile? It's also okay to not notice any positive emotions right now.

> *I wish you peace . . .*
>
> *I wish you health . . .*
>
> *I hope you are without distress, hardship, or misfortune . . .*
>
> *I wish you love and joy . . .*

Take a moment now to shift back to your breath, noticing the rise and fall of your belly with each inhalation and exhalation.

Now bring to mind someone who is a little more difficult. It can be a difficult family member, work colleague, or political figure. It can even be yourself. It should not be anyone who has abused you or was the cause of a trauma. Once you have chosen this individual, imagine them sitting in front of you. Offer them the following statements:

> *I wish to feel at peace or I wish you peace . . .*
>
> *I wish for good health or I wish you health . . .*
>
> *I hope that I am/you are without distress, hardship, and misfortune . . .*
>
> *I wish that I/you experience love and joy . . .*
>
> *. . .*
>
> *I wish to feel at peace or I wish you peace . . .*
>
> *I wish for good health or I wish you health . . .*
>
> *I hope that I am/you are without distress, hardship, and misfortune . . .*
>
> *I wish that I/you experience love and joy . . .*

Notice any emotions or physical feelings that arise.

> *I wish to feel at peace or I wish you peace . . .*
>
> *I wish for good health or I wish you health . . .*
>
> *I hope that I am/you are without distress, hardship, and misfortune . . .*
>
> *I wish that I/you experience love and joy . . .*

Return again to your breath for the next few moments. Take a few deep breaths if you notice yourself being especially distractible.

(continued)

Box 7.1 Continued

Now bring to mind an image of the world, offering positive thoughts.

> *I wish the world peace . . .*

> *I wish the world health . . .*

> *I hope the world is without distress, hardship, or misfortune . . .*

> *I wish the world love and joy . . .*

> *. . .*

> *I wish the world peace . . .*

> *I wish the world health . . .*

> *I hope the world is without distress, hardship, or misfortune . . .*

> *I wish the world love and joy . . .*

Now what emotions and physical symptoms arise?

For the final time, gently shift your attention to your breath . . . and then open your eyes.

Following the practice, ask the client to again rate their mood and then to reflect on the thoughts, emotions, or physical symptoms they noticed. If there were positive emotions or thoughts, highlight the connection between their practice of *Loving-Kindness* and those positive emotions. If there was an improvement in mood, highlight this connection. This will reinforce learning that the practice leads to more positive mood.

If the client had a negative experience, assess the reasons why. Were there feelings of discomfort because it felt awkward or disingenuous? If so, explain that this reaction is expected the first few times they practice *Loving-Kindness*. Did the exercise generate more negative emotions than positive emotions? If so, validate that this often happens if someone chooses a person who is too difficult for the initial practice. If there is sufficient time, have them practice the exercise again with another, less difficult being (e.g., pet). Was the client's mind wandering a lot? If so, validate this experience and explain that one's mind will typically wander less with more practice.

It is essential that you reinforce the principles before moving on to homework. Ask the client what they are taking away from the session or the skill. At a minimum, doing so will help you recognize whether the client has a strong understanding of content and whether some content needs to be reviewed.

Homework for Practicing Loving-Kindness

Clients may photocopy exercises from the workbook or download multiple copies at the Treatments *That Work*™ website (www. oxfordclinicalpsych.com/PAT). For homework, ask your clients to practice the *Loving-Kindness* skill daily, recording their mood before and after on Exercise 7.1. Clients can practice by listening to the audio, reading the script, or recording and listening to themselves read the script.

Case Vignettes for Practicing Loving-Kindness

Case Vignette #1

This vignette demonstrates how the therapist can introduce the skill of *Loving-Kindness*.

T: *Today we are starting a new skill called Loving-Kindness. Have you heard of this practice before?*

C: *No, I don't think so.*

T: *That's not surprising. Loving-Kindness is not a practice that is commonly known in Western cultures. It was originally developed from Buddhist practices as a form of meditation, with Loving-Kindness being one of four sublime states of mind. However, Western medicine has adopted it after recognizing the benefits it has on mental health.*

C: *So, wait, are we doing something religious here, then?*

T: *(smiles) No, this practice is non-religious. It is beneficial whether you are religious or not. How does that sound?*

C: *That sounds good.*

T: *There is a lot of research to show that practicing Loving-Kindness leads to improved mood and reduce negative emotions. For example, one study demonstrated that it led to less anger, pain, and general distress.*

C: *Hmm, cool. Sounds like it could help me.*

T: *Definitely. This is also a great skill to enhance feelings of connection to others. I know that is something you have really been struggling with.*

C: *Yes, I just feel disconnected a lot. It has been better since I started scheduling social activities into my week, but outside of that, it's not a feeling I often have.*

T: *Well, then, this is a fantastic skill for us to practice.*

C: *I'm excited.*

T: *This skill uses imagery.*

C: *Like Imagining the Positive?*

T: *It's a little different. In Loving-Kindness practice, you will visualize a living being or the world more generally. Then you will offer that living being or the world positive thoughts. I will guide you through the visualization and the positive thoughts to offer. While going through the practice, be aware of any thoughts, emotions, or physical sensations that arise. How does all that sound?*

C: *Interesting.*

T: *Fantastic. Would you want to try a practice?*

C: *Yes, sure.*

Case Vignette #2

This vignette demonstrates how to handle situations with clients who struggle to identify an uncomplicated person.

T: *Okay, we have just finished our first Loving-Kindness practice. How did it go for you?*

C: *I couldn't even do it.*

T: *Can you share more of what you mean by that?*

C: *I couldn't do it. You asked me to think of someone who is uncomplicated, and I got stuck there. First, I thought of my mom, but when I did that, I just felt pretty crappy, because I kept thinking of our argument last week. Then, I thought about my sister, but we haven't talked in years. Then, I thought about my dad, and you know that history. . . . And, then I had trouble thinking about anyone else.*

T: *It seems that you really did get stuck. Many people can get stuck here. Your struggle to find an uncomplicated person highlights how complicated people can be. Other people can bring up a lot of mixed emotions, especially people closest to us.*

C: *I can definitely see that with my family. I'm glad that it's not just me.*

T: *It's definitely not just you. When this happens, a helpful step forward is to figure out who you will choose before you even start the practice. We can figure that out together.*

C: *Okay.*

T: *Your mom, dad, and sister all feel too complicated right now. Is there anyone else in your family, like a distant relative, who might feel less complicated? For example, many people find that grandparents can be easier to practice this skill with than other family members.*

C: *My grandparents aren't living anymore, and I didn't really know them when they were alive.*

T: *Okay. Well, actually, to do this exercise, they do not need to be alive. Also, you can still choose them even if you didn't know them, but sometimes it's more helpful to start with someone you did know.*

C: *I don't know of anyone else in my family.*

T: *What about someone outside of your family? Are there any friends who feel less complicated?*

C: *I don't feel like I have any friends.*

T: *I know that's something we worked on earlier in this treatment. You scheduled social activities where you met new people and continued to interact with them. Even if you don't yet consider them friends, they may be good candidates for this practice.*

C: *How would I know if they are good candidates?*

T: *Great question. Do they bring up any strong negative emotions for you when you think about them?*

C: *No.*

T: *Okay, that already makes them possible good candidates for earlier practices. Although you can practice Loving-Kindness with anyone, including those who bring up many negative feelings, it is easier to start with someone who brings up little to no negative emotions. Another requirement is that you can imagine their face or their name. Can you remember either their face or name?*

C:	Yes.
T:	*Fabulous. It sounds like any of those friends or individuals would be good candidates. Other possibilities are an old mentor or teacher, an old friend, a pet, or stranger toward whom you feel compassion or other positive emotions.*
C:	*I can choose my dog, or I can choose that really nice older woman who started talking to me while waiting in line at the grocery store.*
T:	*Either of those would be wonderful options. Which of these individuals would you like to choose for our next practice?*
C:	*Can we start with my dog?*
T:	*Absolutely.*

Troubleshooting for Practicing Loving-Kindness

The most common difficulty is experiencing negative emotions with the *Loving-Kindness* exercises. Clients may report feeling jealousy, anger, sadness, or irritation. These are normal reactions, especially if the person they identified for the practice is someone with whom there have been strained relations. It is important to first normalize the client's reaction. If there is sufficient time in session, you can lead another practice, encouraging the client to choose someone less difficult (e.g., a pet, a houseplant, a teacher/mentor they once loved) to see if different emotions arise. Finally, explain to the client that it can often take multiple practices (even weeks or months) before they experience positive emotions, which is why we recommend practicing these skills repeatedly and sometimes for extended time periods.

Another common response is feelings of awkwardness or being disingenuous. Validate this experience, and explain that over time these feelings will dissipate.

Another client problem may be that they have no one who is uncomplicated in their life; maybe everyone they interact with generates some negative feelings. If this is the case, see if the client can practice these exercises with a pet, a houseplant, or a person from their past with whom they no longer interact.

Background

Gratitude is polysemy (i.e., having multiple definitions); it is an emotion, behavior, and thought strategy. Wood and colleagues (2008c, 2010) have suggested the following definitions: recognition and appreciation of the positive, an appreciation of other people, a focus on one's possessions, admiration for beauty, a behavioral expression, mindful awareness of the positive, appreciation that one's life is time-limited, and a healthy comparison to those less fortunate.

From an evolutionary perspective, *Gratitude* may be a function of maintaining social connectedness. Indeed, it is believed to be a practice that explains why humans exhibit reciprocal altruism (Trivers, 1971), where an organism behaves in a way that undermines its own strength to enhance the strength of another organism (and the expectation that this will be reciprocated).

Of all the skills discussed in this chapter, *Gratitude* has been studied the most. Research has demonstrated associations between *Gratitude* and a number of beneficial mental health outcomes, such as lower levels of stress and depression (Wood et al., 2008c). *Gratitude* is also associated with positive affect (Emmons & McCullough, 2003; McCullough et al., 2002), including emotions of happiness (McCullough et al., 2002; Van Overwalle et al., 1995), pride (Van Overwalle et al., 1995), hope (Van Overwalle et al., 1995), and optimism (Emmons & McCullough, 2003; McCullough et al., 2002).

In addition, *Gratitude* has positive interpersonal benefits, including improved relationships (Algoe & Haidt, 2009), prosocial behavior (Emmons & McCullough, 2003), greater willingness to forgive (DeShea, 2003), enhanced feelings of connectedness with others (Emmons & McCullough, 2003; McCullough et al., 2002), and heightened levels of perceived support (Wood et al., 2008b). More generally, research has demonstrated the association between *Gratitude* and positive well-being (Emmons & McCullough, 2003; McCullough et al., 2002). As a treatment skill, *Gratitude* is defined as: (1) the act of recognizing and appreciating something positive in this world, or (2) thinking about what one appreciates.

The goal of *Gratitude* as an intervention is to target noticing and appreciating the positive, as part of attainment of reward, or liking. One study found that positive appraisals of aid received mediated the relationship between state and trait *Gratitude*, which may explain why grateful people tend to feel more *Gratitude* after receiving aid. However, some research suggests that anticipation and learning of reward are implicated in *Gratitude* (Fox et al., 2015; Wood et al., 2010).

How to Practice Gratitude

After reviewing the science and history of *Gratitude*, lead your client through a practice of *Gratitude* in session. This will help the client better understand how to complete the homework.

One of the best *Gratitude* interventions is creating a *Gratitude* list. There are many ways to create such lists; however, in this treatment, we have the client make an ongoing list of unique things they are grateful for each day. To start, guide the client to use the Exercise 7.2: Gratitude list, which can be found in the client workbook and also in the appendix at the end of this therapist guide. Ask the client to record five unique things (different from the prior day) that they were grateful for yesterday, ensuring that they rate their mood beforehand and afterward. Clients may photocopy this exercise from the workbook or download multiple copies at the Treatments *That Work*™ website (www. oxfordclinicalpsych.com/PAT).

Clients may struggle here. If you notice this, ask the client to use *Finding the Silver Linings* to identify positive aspects of yesterday. If they continue to struggle, you can remind them that the silver lining need not be big; it can be small and even silly.

Once the client has identified five unique *Gratitude* items for yesterday and written them down on their exercise form, have them rate their mood again. Then discuss with the client what they noticed when practicing this skill. Ensure that they understand the rationale of the skill. Ultimately, the client will generate at least 35 unique items of things they are grateful for each week. Thinking about things we are grateful for and reviewing the cumulative list are great ways to boost mood. Check to see if clients notice this already in their own mood ratings.

Homework for Practicing Gratitude

Clients may photocopy exercises from the workbook or download multiple copies at the Treatments *That Work*™ website (www.oxfordclinicalpsych.com/PAT). For homework, ask your clients to record five unique things they are grateful for each day, listing them on Exercise 7.2: Gratitude. It might be helpful to encourage clients to identify a time of day to practice and have them set a reminder on their phone. This increases the likelihood that they will follow through each day and that it will become routine.

Case Vignettes for Practicing Gratitude

Case Vignette #1

This vignette demonstrates how to handle situations with clients who struggle to identify *Gratitude* items.

T: *Let's start with a practice. See if you can write down five things you are grateful for from yesterday.*

C: *Okay, but I'm pretty sure there's nothing. Yesterday was pretty crappy.*

T: *I'm sorry to hear that yesterday was rough. Would you be willing to give it a good effort and then we can talk about it?*

C: *Okay.* (thinking, fiddling with his pencil, and then gives up within a minute) *I don't know. I can't think of anything. I just keep on thinking about how shitty my day was. I can't believe that after I got locked out of my house, my brother took two hours to get over to my place to give me the spare key. I just sat out there, bored out of my mind. And of course, it started raining.*

T: *I'm sorry that yesterday was so difficult, and I can tell that you are getting stuck in that right now.*

C: *Ugh, yes.*

T: *Let's see if we can make this easier by starting with a day that was a decent day. Is there any day this week that you could consider decent?*

C: Today has been okay.

T: That's great! Let's go with today. What is at least one thing you can think of to be grateful for today?

C: (thinking for a few seconds and then gives up) I really don't know.

T: I noticed that you thought about it for less than a minute. Let's try to give it some more time to think of at least one thing you are grateful for.

C: Okay. (thinking for a couple of minutes) I guess I'm grateful for not being locked out of my house today.

T: That's great! Let's go with that. Can you write that down as one thing to be grateful for today?

C: Oh, okay. (client writes)

T: What else?

C: I really don't know.

T: Sometimes when we get stuck, it can be helpful to try silver linings.

C: So what's my situation?

T: The situation can be today. Or, if you want to get more specific, it can be sitting in therapy today.

C: Okay, I'll go with sitting in therapy today as the situation.

T: Fantastic.

C: Well, one silver lining of sitting in therapy today is that I get to speak with you, which usually makes me feel better. Another is that I am learning something new. I guess one more is that I managed to get here on time so that I could get the full session.

T: These are all great! You now have four gratitude items for today so far.

C: Oh, I see. Okay, my silver linings are also things to be grateful for.

T: Precisely.

C: Okay, but I really can't think of anything else.

T: Another helpful tool when getting stuck is to think of things you have that others might not. These can be really basic, like having a home to live in. It might be having money for food, being able to see, hear, and speak, being able to walk and use your arms . . .

C: Okay, I get the point. So there are actually a lot more than five things I can write down for today.

T: There are, and what we are doing today and over the next week is training your brain to start noticing things to be grateful for in order to elicit that feeling of gratitude, which has a lot of beneficial effects on our well-being.

C: Makes sense. I think I get it now.

T: Fantastic.

Case Vignette #2

This vignette demonstrates how to respond to clients who struggled with this assignment for homework.

C: *I kind of did my homework this week. I tried.*

T: *Well, that's great. Let's see what you've got.*

C: *I tried doing two gratitude exercises, and then I gave up.*

T: *Hmm, okay, we will definitely talk through it to figure out what happened. Either way, can I take a look at your exercise sheets?*

C: *Here you go.*

T: *I can see here that on Friday you wrote down three things you were grateful for, and then only two things the next day, and nothing after that. Is that right?*

C: *Yeah, I'm sorry.*

T: *That's okay. What do you think might have happened?*

C: *I had a really hard time coming up with as many as five things I was grateful for on Friday. Then, on Saturday, it was even harder for me to think of things to be grateful for that were different from Friday. So I just gave up after that.*

T: *It sounds like you gave it a good effort. However, the assignment might have been a little too difficult to start with.*

C: *Maybe.*

T: *Okay, let's adjust the assignment so that it's more manageable, and then over time you can work back up to five gratitude items per day.*

C: *Is five a special number?*

T: (smiles) *No, in fact you never have to work your way up to five items per day. It's an arbitrary number that is intended to train your mind to notice the positive more. That said, since you managed to identify two or three items on Friday and Saturday, let's see if we can start with two unique gratitude items per day.*

C: *I think I can do that. Basically, I have to come up with two things per day that I am grateful for that are different from the prior day.*

T: *Exactly. In fact, let's practice in session, by writing out two gratitude items for as many days of last week as you can remember. We can start with yesterday. What are two things you might have been grateful for yesterday?*

C: *Okay, um, I was really grateful that my husband cooked dinner for me. It really helped reduce some of my stress.*

T: *Fabulous. Let's write that down. What else?*

C: *I was also really grateful that I had time to go for a long walk that morning.*

T: *Great. Now what about Wednesday? What were two things you were grateful for that day?*

C: *That's when my boss gave me the positive feedback on my report. I was really appreciative that he took the time to do that. Also, I was grateful that I didn't have to redo the report.*

T: *Fantastic. Let's see if we can try the day before that too.*

C: *On Tuesday? That was a while ago. Hmm, I'm really not sure. I can't remember Tuesday all that well. I went to work that day and didn't do much in the evening. I really can't remember anything significant. I guess I can be grateful that nothing eventful happened.*

T: *Absolutely. And we can stop there. Do you feel more comfortable with the homework now?*

C: *Yes, definitely.*

T: *Would you be willing to try that this week?*

Case Vignette #3

This vignette demonstrates how to practice this skill with clients who have considerable hardships and believe that they have nothing to be grateful for.

T: *Let's try a practice of Gratitude. On your exercise sheet, see if you can write down five things you are grateful for in the last day. But before you do that, go ahead and rate your mood on a 0-to-10 scale.*

C: *Okay. I guess I'm at a 4 out of 10 right now . . . (writing) . . . As for five things I'm grateful for, I have no idea. . . . Um, I don't know. In fact, maybe I'm at 2 out of 10 for my mood.*

T: *It sounds like your mood just decreased when thinking about the practice.*

C: *It did*

T: *What's coming up for you?*

C: *I really don't think I have things to be grateful for right now. I'm un-employed. I can barely pay the bills. I basically have no friends. My sister won't talk to me. I'm never good enough for my mother. And, my father never cared about me.*

T: *That's a lot. I can imagine that when you think of all that, your mood understandably decreases.*

C: *Yeah.*

T: *You've had some definite hardships in your life, especially more recently. That's undeniable, and it's important to acknowledge that. At the same time, getting stuck or dwelling on those hardships is problematic. Do you feel like you might be dwelling on these negative experiences?*

C: *I guess so.*

T: *That's something that happens often, isn't it?*

C: *Yes, it happens like all the time.*

T: *I thought so. In fact, that's one of the primary reasons you came to this treatment. You were dwelling on the past and experiencing a lot of depression.*

C: *All of that's true.*

T: *So in this treatment, we are going to try something different. Would you be willing to try something new?*

C: *Okay.*

T: *We are going to practice stretching your brain to start noticing things that you can be grateful for each day. Science has shown again and again how helpful doing this is for our mood.*

C: *That sounds like silver linings.*

T: *It is very similar to silver linings. In fact, we can use silver linings to help identify Gratitude items.*

C: *Okay.*

T: *Like silver linings, Gratitude items can be big, small, or even silly. What is one small thing that you might be grateful for today?*

C: *I still really don't know.*

T: *That's okay. One really helpful way to identify gratitude items is to think of things you have that others might not have or that you previously did not have.*

C: *Like what? I feel like others have plenty of things that I don't.*

T: *Some definitely do. Think basic needs. What are some basic human needs?*

C: *Air, food, shelter, and water.*

T: *Great. Those are actually four things you can identify being grateful for today. You have clean air to breathe and clean water to drink. You can also feed yourself and have a place to live.*

C: *I guess all of that is true.*

T: *Also, sometimes we take for granted basic functioning. For example, we forget that not everyone has all four limbs or the ability to see or hear. These are also things to be grateful for.*

C: *I see.*

T: *Sometimes it's best to start with these items, and as you practice this skill more, you might start noticing other things to be grateful for every day. For example, you might start noticing that there was more wildlife on your walk, which you were grateful for. Or maybe you forgot to look up something on your computer before you left the house, and you are grateful that you could look up the answer on your phone without going back home.*

C: *Okay, I get it. One thing I can be grateful for today is that I have therapy to go to.*

T: (smiles) *Precisely.*

Troubleshooting for Practicing Gratitude

With the skill of *Gratitude*, a common difficulty will be clients who suggest that they have nothing for which to be grateful. Many clients feel depressed because of their considerable hardships. It is important to be validating of this and practice small downward comparisons with them. Adding basic needs and functioning to the *Gratitude* list can help clients realize that there are always some things for which to be grateful. These might include still being alive, ability to see and hear, ability to walk or use one's arms, ability to attend therapy and receive medical care, having shelter over one's head, ability to pay for food, and having some support in their lives. There are many examples of this. Encourage clients to be creative. Also, returning to the skill of *Finding the Silver Linings* can be helpful for this.

Another common difficulty is struggling to identify as many as five things clients are grateful for each day. The number of *Gratitude* items per day can be adjusted to the client. If the client is really struggling to identify five items per day, they can start with one or two items and build up from there.

Background

Generosity is the act of giving by choice without expecting something in return. It is not limited to material goods, even though it is typically perceived this way; *Generosity* can be giving of one's time, energy, knowledge, or other resources.

Humans have engaged in generous and altruistic behavior since possibly the origin of humankind. Indeed, sociological studies have found that *Generosity* is cross-cultural and occurs across age groups (Aknin et al., 2015). However, our understanding of why humans across cultures and history engage in generous acts is limited to theories. Some theories state that generous behavior improves partner selection (Hamilton, 1963), enhances one's reputation (Bénabou & Tirole, 2006), and increases the likelihood of receiving help (Trivers, 1971).

There is important evidence to support the theory that humans evolved with generous behavior to ensure they receive help when needed. Current research has demonstrated that spending money on others predicts increased happiness (Dunn et al., 2008), and acts of kindness are reported more by happier people (Otake et al., 2006). Further, generosity has been found to be socially contagious (Tsvetkova & Macy, 2014), in that one is more likely to be generous when experiencing a generous act.

It has been suggested that activities like *Generosity* protect against risk for negative outcomes (Layous et al., 2014). In one study, daily prosocial behavior moderated the effects of stress on affect (Raposa et al., 2016). Indeed, research more generally has demonstrated a link between *Generosity* and positive outcomes, especially when *Generosity* is in the form of volunteering. Those positive outcomes include positive affect (Aknin et al., 2015; Otake et al., 2006), greater well-being (Borgonovi, 2008; Thoits & Hewitt, 2001), lower mortality rates (Musick et al., 1999; Oman et al., 1999), and decreased depression (Musick & Wilson, 2003).

In PAT, *Generosity* is used to target the attainment of reward, or liking, and learning of reward. Research into the mechanisms of *Generosity* has found that tweaking oxytocin levels (Zak et al., 2007), disrupting dorsolateral and dorsomedial prefrontal cortical functioning (Christov-Moore et al., 2017), and MDMA administration (Kirkpatrick et al., 2015) result in enhanced *Generosity*.

How to Practice Generosity

It will be largely impractical for clients to practice an actual act of *Generosity* in session—although there may be exceptions that can be done in session, such as the client texting a friend and offering to help with something. Therefore, dedicate most of the session practice to generating a thorough list of *Generosity* activities clients can do over the following week.

Remind clients that *Generosity* need not be material, even though this is often how we think of it. *Generosity* can be free of monetary cost and unconstrained by time and energy when we think of it in creative ways. For example, it can take the form of time, energy, knowledge, and other resources. It also is worth discussing with the client that *Generosity* need not be toward another person; we can also be generous toward ourselves, animals, and the world.

Have the client generate a list of generous acts that they could do, using Exercise 7.3: Generosity, which can be found in the client workbook and also in the appendix at the end of this therapist guide. Ensure that these activities include both material and non-material activities. Ten to 20 items are a good amount, and encourage clients to continue adding to this list. Instruct clients to rate their mood before and after each act of *Generosity*, and ask them to notice how their mood state changes as a result of engaging in *Generosity* in order to deepen reward learning (i.e., their actions produced more positive mood).

Homework for Practicing Generosity

Clients may photocopy exercises from the workbook or download multiple copies at the Treatments *That Work*™ website (www.oxfordclinicalpsych.com/PAT). For homework, ask your clients to practice three acts of *Generosity* this week to be recorded on the Exercise 7.3: Generosity sheets, along with the day(s) they plan to complete them. Scheduling these activities in advance will increase the likelihood that they are completed. One exercise form/sheet will be used for each act of generosity.

Case Vignettes for Practicing Generosity

Case Vignette #1

This vignette demonstrates how to respond to a client who fears they do not have enough time or resources to be generous.

C: *I understand that being generous is really important. I wish I was more generous. But I feel like I can't be more generous. Does that make me a bad person?*

T: *Absolutely not. Let's talk through what you mean by "can't be more generous."*

C: *Well, I feel like I can't. I want to be. I really do, but I'm so tired, and money is tight, and I don't know . . .*

T: *I'm hearing that you feel like you have nothing left to give.*

C: *Yes, that's exactly right! I wish I could give my time, but I already feel busy. I wish I could give money, but I also know it's important for me to save for my retirement. I also would love to give coworkers more effort, but I already feel so drained.*

T: *That all makes sense. A lot of people feel this way. They fear giving, because they believe that they don't have enough to give.*

C: *Yes. That's me.*

T: *When we think of Generosity in the traditional sense, not having enough can be a reality. We may not have money to give. Or we may not have the time to help someone move into a new home. Or we may be too drained to call a friend and listen to their day.*

C: *So it's not just me.*

T: *Definitely not. We all have our limitations.*

C: *I'm glad to hear this, but I am also disappointed that I am not able to be more generous, especially if it's supposed to help me too.*

T: *The great news is that anyone can be more generous if we look at Generosity differently. Traditionally, people think of Generosity as money, physical help, or time and energy.*

C: *That's the way I think of it.*

T: *That's not surprising. In the traditional sense, Generosity is limited. However, Generosity can be viewed as limitless if you consider it in limitless ways. In addition to time, physical help, objects, and money, Generosity can be in the form of knowledge, advice, feedback, comfort, validation, a smile, love, care, compassion, and empathy.*

C: *I guess I never thought of those other ways to be generous.*

T: *Generosity can be toward other people, but it can also be toward one's self, animals, or the world more generally. Anyone and anything can be the recipient of Generosity. In these ways, Generosity can be limitless.*

C: *I can see that.*

T: *Can you think of one example of a way that you can be generous this week despite being so busy and tired?*

C: *I can hug my daughter or smile at a colleague.*

T: *Great ideas.*

C: *I guess I can also try to garden more, which I love, because that would be giving something back to the world.*

T: *Absolutely.*

C: *Would making eco-friendly choices, like buying more eco-friendly products instead of alternatives, be another example?*

T: *For sure. Generosity can take countless forms and can look different for each individual who engages in the practice.*

C: *Okay, I get it now.*

Case Vignette #2

This vignette demonstrates how to respond to clients who avoid being generous because they fear their *Generosity* will not be appreciated.

C: *I didn't do my homework again. It was just too hard.*

T: *Well, let's definitely talk about that. I'm assuming you're referring to the Generosity assignment?*

C: *Yes, the one where I was supposed to cook for my mom and bring her food.*

T: *I remember. What do you think made the activity so difficult?*

C: *I don't know. It just was.*

T: *Was there not enough time to cook? Or did cooking for someone else feel overwhelming?*

C: *No, neither. I actually cooked the meal, and I was about to head out the door to surprise my mom with it.*

T: *What happened then?*

C: I remembered the last time I did something nice for her.

T: What happened the last time you did something nice for her?

C: She didn't seem to care. I figured this time would be the same.

T: You were afraid that your Generosity wouldn't be appreciated.

C: Yeah, exactly. A few months ago, I tried to clean up my mom's garage, and she didn't even say "thank you." I don't even know if she noticed.

T: That sounds like it was very frustrating and hurtful.

C: It was! I put so much effort into it. I would have liked some recognition.

T: You are not alone in feeling hurt by generous deeds not being noticed or appreciated. Generosity requires us to give some of our resources, making us vulnerable.

C: I hate feeling vulnerable.

T: Most people do. People don't like to feel exposed and open to hurt.

C: Right.

T: At the same time, sometimes we have to feel vulnerability to achieve our goals. For example, you felt some vulnerability scheduling those social activities earlier in treatment, and yet by doing so, you developed more friendships.

C: I did.

T: In the same way, feeling vulnerable and hurt might be a side effect of doing a generous deed sometimes. However, the payout is the possibility of increasing your mood overall and feeling more positive emotions, like pride, love, compassion, and appreciative joy, which is something we will learn next week.

C: I'm not sure it's worth it.

T: I remember you saying the same thing about social activities. (smiles) Did you find doing those social activities worth it?

C: They were. I can give this a shot. But does that mean I have to feel bad every time I am generous?

T: Just shifting your view of what Generosity is can lessen some of the hurt if the deed is not appreciated.

C: How?

T: Remember, we defined Generosity as "giving without expecting in return." When we do that, the generous deed is not about the outcome but rather about the activity itself. It's doing something not to achieve a goal but to do it because it is important. An example of this is your daily walks. From what I heard you say, you don't go on your daily walks to lose weight, you walk every day because it's important to you.

C: That's right. Okay, I think I get it.

For *Generosity*, the most common concern among clients is not having the time or resources to perform generous acts. Validate this and explain that *Generosity* need not take much—or any—of one's resources. An act of *Generosity* can be smiling at someone, thinking a positive thought, offering a piece of advice, actively listening, or letting someone borrow something. It can be toward another person, a pet, or toward the world. It can also be an act of self-care. Ensure that clients understand that sometimes we find ourselves doing too much for others and not enough for ourselves. When this happens, acts of generosity should be dedicated to oneself.

Another common concern about *Generosity* is that something would not be appreciated if given. This is a very likely outcome of *Generosity* that you should acknowledge. At the same time, it is important to remind clients that we cannot control other people's behavior. Also, explain that research shows that the act of giving, regardless of whether it is appreciated, has benefits. If clients are still struggling with not receiving appreciation, highlight their choice of giving something with openness versus an expectation of appreciation. The latter is likely to lead to feelings of regret and resentment.

Practicing Appreciative Joy

Background

Appreciative Joy is the experience of positive emotions that emerge from the success of others (Grossman, 2015; Zeng et al., 2017). It is also a practice that is intended to generate these types of emotions. Like *Loving-Kindness*, *Appreciative Joy* stems from Eastern spiritual practices and is identified as one of four states of wholesomeness in the Buddhist tradition (Grossman, 2015).

During the practice, one offers positive thoughts of continued good fortune to another, while being aware of emotions, thoughts, and physical symptoms that arise. Unlike *Loving-Kindness*, clients begin by thinking of someone who recently had fortune or success come to them and offering them additional or continued fortune.

There is evidence to suggest that *Appreciative Joy* has a beneficial effect on mental health outcomes. For example, more experiences of appreciative joy have been associated with more positive emotions, life satisfaction, and trait happiness (Zeng et al., 2017). More generally, *Appreciative Joy* enhances feelings of connectedness.

In PAT, *Appreciative Joy* is designed to target the attainment of reward, or liking.

How to Practice Appreciative Joy

As with *Loving-Kindness*, the client practices an *Appreciative Joy* exercise with you in session. You will lead the client through this exercise in session to allow for processing and troubleshooting, by reading the guided instructions script in Box 7.2. Ensure that the client records their mood beforehand using the Exercise 7.4: Appreciative Joy form, which can be found in the client workbook and also in the appendix at the end of this therapist guide. Note that a 🔊 recording of the script is available for both you and your clients on the Treatments *That Work*™ website (www. oxfordclinicalpsych.com/PAT), and clients may photocopy this exercise from the workbook or download multiple copies from the website.

Box 7.2 Guided Instructions for Practicing Appreciative Joy

Find a comfortable position someplace with little to no distractions. It can be helpful to sit in a chair with your feet flat on the ground, your back upright, and your eyes closed or gently resting on a spot in front of you.

If you notice that your mind is racing, wandering, or being especially distractible today, take a moment to gently shift your attention to your breath, by noticing each inhalation and each exhalation. Observe the changes in your body as you take air in and as you release it. Notice your belly rising and falling or the change in temperature of the air traveling in and out of your nose.

Whenever you are ready, begin by identifying someone who you like and who is uncomplicated. This can be someone who you deeply care about, even a pet, or it can be someone who you know from a distance but greatly respect. Imagine them sitting in front of you, smiling, and looking back at you.

Identify one good fortune that they have. Notice the emotions that arise as you identify what that is.

(continued)

Box 7.2 Continued

Offer them the following statements, focusing on the words as you say them aloud or in your mind:

I am happy you are happy and content . . .

I hope your success stays with you . . .

I hope your wealth continues to grow . . .

. . .

I am happy you are happy and content . . .

I hope your success stays with you . . .

I hope your wealth continues to grow . . .

Notice what emotions and physical sensations emerge as you offer these statements. Joy? A smile? It's also okay to not have any positive emotions right now.

Take a moment to shift back to your breath, noticing the rise and fall of your belly with each inhalation and exhalation.

Now bring to mind someone who is a little more difficult. It can be yourself, a friend, or a family member. Once you have chosen this individual, imagine them sitting in front of you.

Identify one good fortune that they have. Notice the emotions that arise as you identify what that is. Offer them the following statements:

I am happy you are happy and content . . .

I hope your success stays with you . . .

I hope your wealth continues to grow . . .

. . .

I am happy you are happy and content . . .

I hope your success stays with you . . .

I hope your wealth continues to grow . . .

Notice any emotions or physical feelings that arise.

For the final time, gently shift your attention to your breath . . . and then open your eyes.

Following the practice, the client again rates their mood. Then process their experience by asking about the thoughts, emotions, or physical symptoms they noticed. If the client experienced positive emotions or thoughts, highlight the connection between their practice of *Appreciative Joy* and those positive emotions. If there was an improvement in mood, highlight this connection. This will reinforce learning that the practice leads to more positive mood.

If the client had a negative experience, assess the reasons why. Were there feelings of discomfort because it felt awkward or disingenuous? If so, explain that this is expected the first few times they practice *Appreciative Joy*. Did this exercise generate more negative emotions than positive emotions? If so, validate that this often happens if someone chooses a person who is too difficult for the initial practice. If there is sufficient time, have them practice the exercise again with another, less difficult being (e.g., pet). Was their mind wandering a lot? If so, validate this experience and explain that one's mind will typically wander less with more practice.

Homework for Practicing Appreciative Joy

Clients may photocopy exercises from the workbook or download multiple copies at the Treatments *That Work*^{TM} website (www.oxfordclinicalpsych. com/PAT). For homework, ask your clients to practice the *Appreciative Joy* exercise daily, recording their mood before and after on Exercise 7.4. Clients can practice by listening to the audio, reading the script, or recording and listening to themselves reading the script.

Case Vignettes for Practicing Appreciative Joy

Case Vignette #1

The following vignette demonstrates how you can introduce *Appreciative Joy*.

T: *The final skill is Appreciative Joy. Is Appreciative Joy something you've heard of before?*

C: *No, I've never heard of Appreciative—what was it?*

T: (smiles) *Appreciative Joy. Appreciative Joy is both a practice and an emotion. It is the feeling of joy or other positive emotions as a result of the joy that someone else experiences. It is also a skill we practice to cultivate that emotion.*

C: *Cultivate? What does that mean?*

T: *Cultivate means to foster or promote growth of. Basically, this is a skill you will practice that will hopefully bring on more positive feelings over time.*

C: *Oh, I see. So this is a joy that we feel from someone else's joy.*

T: *Exactly. Have you ever experienced that before—feeling joy or positive emotions as a result of seeing someone else experience a positive emotion?*

C: *It would happen all of the time with my daughter when she was a little girl. She would get so happy opening presents, riding her bike, or snuggling up next to our golden retriever that I couldn't help but smile, knowing that she was so happy.*

T: *I am noticing that you are even smiling right now as you talk about it.*

C: *Oh! I guess I am! So, yes, I've definitely experienced Appreciative Joy. I just didn't know there was a name for it.*

T: *Most people are not familiar with the name. Like Loving-Kindness, it was originally developed as a form of meditation in Buddhist practice. And, also like Loving-Kindness, there is research showing that practicing Appreciative Joy leads to more positive emotions, especially connectedness.*

C: *I can see that. Well, I really liked Loving-Kindness, so I think I'll like this too.*

T: *Great. The practice is very similar. Would you be willing to try a practice right now?*

C: *That sounds great.*

Case Vignette #2

This vignette demonstrates how to handle situations with clients who only feel negative emotions during a practice of *Appreciative Joy.*

T: *Now that we've completed your first practice of Appreciative Joy, what did you notice?*

C: *Ugh, that did not go well.*

T: *Can you tell me more?*

C: *I just feel bad after doing it.*

T: Okay, it sounds like the practice brought up some negative emotions. Can you identify or label at least one specific negative emotion you experienced during the practice?

C: Definitely jealousy . . . and shame.

T: Those are certainly difficult negative emotions.

C: They are.

T: Well, it might be helpful to better understand what led to those negative emotions in the practice. What person did you identify for the practice?

C: My best friend from childhood.

T: Okay, and were you able to bring an image of his face to mind?

C: I did—pretty vividly, too. But as soon as I started offering him those statements, I started imagining all of his fortune, and that got me thinking about everything I don't have. Like, he has a wife, kids, a huge house, and a great job. I'm unemployed and can barely pay my studio apartment rent. I am such a failure.

T: It sounds like you went down a downward spiral during this exercise.

C: Definitely.

T: It is not uncommon for this practice to bring up some negative emotions. In fact, part of this practice is noticing and acknowledging any emotions—positive or negative—that emerge. The intention is not to change them, but rather to just observe them, as difficult as this might be.

C: I remember—it was the same with Loving-Kindness. It's only after lots of practice that we might notice feeling better.

T: Exactly.

C: But I liked Loving-Kindness a lot better. It typically made me feel calm. This one didn't.

T: I'm wondering if part of the reason you reacted so strongly to this exercise is that you were assuming joy or fortune is limited. Do you remember our discussion of Generosity?

C: That if I think of Generosity as limited, it can be hard to be generous. However, if I think of it as unlimited, it is easier to find ways to give.

T: Precisely. That was a really nice summary. Appreciative Joy is the same. It can be easier to generate positive feelings toward another for their joy and fortune if we recognize that someone else's fortune does not affect our own.

C: Like maybe one day we both can own our own homes and have a family? And one day, I will hopefully get a job too.

T: Exactly. Also, when feelings of jealousy emerge from an Appreciative Joy practice, Gratitude can be a helpful skill to practice.

C: That makes sense. And I do have a good amount to be grateful for.

T: Let's try one more thing. Instead of choosing your friend, who might be too complicated for your first practice, let's choose someone less complicated for your next practice. Is there someone or some pet you can't help but feel joy when they are happy?

C: My dog. She is so funny when she gets excited. She starts running and jumping around and licking my face. I love seeing her happy.

T: Wonderful. Let's do this practice with her next.

Troubleshooting for Practicing Appreciative Joy

The most common client difficulty in learning the skill of *Appreciative Joy* is experiencing negative emotions with the exercises. Clients may report feeling jealousy, anger, sadness, or irritation. These are normal reactions, especially if the person they identified for the exercise is someone who is "difficult" for a variety of reasons. It is important to first normalize the client's reaction. If there is sufficient time in session, you can lead another practice, encouraging the client to choose someone less difficult (e.g., a pet, a teacher/mentor they once loved) to see if different emotions arise. Finally, explain to the client that it can often take multiple practices (even weeks or months) before they experience positive emotions, which is why we recommend practicing these skills repeatedly and sometimes for extended time periods.

Other common responses to *Appreciative Joy* exercises (similar to *Loving-Kindness*) are feelings of awkwardness or being disingenuous. Validate this experience, and explain that over time these feelings will dissipate. Also, clients can choose to modify the statements that are offered during the practice of *Appreciative Joy* to better reflect what they are able to think or feel (e.g., "I am glad that you are doing well").

Clients sometimes report that they have no one who is uncomplicated in their lives; maybe everyone with whom they interact generates some negative feelings. If this is case, see if they can practice these exercises with a pet, a houseplant, or a person from their past who they may no longer interact with.

Treatment Gains and Relapse Prevention

CHAPTER 8

Continuing the Journey After Treatment

(Corresponds to chapter 8 of client workbook)

Materials Needed

- Exercise 8.1: My Progress Assessment (all exercises are included in the client workbook and also included in the appendix at the end of this therapist guide)
- Exercise 8.2: My Long-Term Goals
- Exercise 8.3: Maintaining My Gains
- Exercise 8.4: Overcoming Barriers

Goals

- Review content from last session and answer any questions.
- Identify and review treatment gains.
- Review long-term goals.
- Discuss and troubleshoot continued practice barriers.
- Discuss how to manage "high-risk" times (lapse vs. relapse).

Summary of Information in Chapter 8 of Client Workbook

- Evidence suggests that continued practice is an essential aspect of maintaining therapy gains.
- Identifying long-term goals promotes continued practice after treatment has ended.
- Making plans for overcoming barriers help clients anticipate and cope with circumstances that prevent ongoing skill training.
- A lapse is a temporary return of symptoms, whereas a relapse is a return to the pretreatment baseline. High-risk times or triggers can facilitate lapse/relapse. Awareness and a management plan can reduce the likelihood of lapse/relapse.

Key Concepts

The key concept of this chapter is to prepare clients for treatment termination. The final session is dedicated to reviewing the client's progress, identifying long-term treatment goals, and identifying strategies to maintain gains and cope with difficult times. You will reinforce the idea of continued practice to maintain and refine treatment gains. Assessing barriers can help clients cope with difficult times. Educate your clients on the difference between lapse and relapse and reinforce the benefits of continued practice and awareness of stressful triggers to maintain a positive mood cycle and upward spirals. Goals for the client are to:

- Begin the process of independent practice.
- Review and identify treatment gains and long-term goals.
- Build a plan on how to troubleshoot difficult times and barriers.
- Understand and appreciate the difference between lapse and relapse.

Clients respond differently to the end of treatment: Some look forward to the last session, while others experience discomfort or even fear. Assure the client that this is natural. As with most skills, we learn with the support of someone else, it can be scary to continue without that person's help and presence in our lives. Be aware of negative thoughts common in individuals with emotional disorders such as, "I cannot do this on my own," "I will relapse without my therapist's help," or "there are skills I have not mastered yet." Activities in this chapter are designed to combat those thoughts by assisting the client to develop a sense of ownership and mastery. It is essential to start reminding clients that treatment is coming to an end at least two weeks before the last session. As discussed in this chapter, ending treatment marks the beginning of continued practice. It is by no means an end to learning and continuous improvement.

Begin the last session by complimenting your client for completing the Positive Affect Treatment (PAT). Take a moment and help your client pause, notice, and appreciate the steps they have taken and the efforts they have made over the last several months. Remind them to take ownership of their work and give themselves praise for it. Ask them about their positive feelings as they do so. Do they feel pride, excitement, and a sense of ownership? Have them savor their accomplishments!

Next, review client progress to determine the skills they have mastered and the ones that require further work. As you review the questions in Exercise 8.1: My Progress Assessment, remind clients that progress is rarely linear.

Progress is assessed most accurately by examining the objective change in the weekly scores on the standardized questionnaires rather than asking clients how they feel. Explain how fluctuations in the scores can be confusing and feel uncomfortable but are common and expected. Discuss how the data serves as one source of information about the client's progress rather than being an indicator of who they are. Remind your client that treatment does not take place in a vacuum: Changes in life circumstances, health, and society are expected to influence one's mood. Treatment gains—increases in positive mood and decreases in negative mood—will help temper the impact of internal and external influences.

Encourage clients to take ownership of their effort and the energy they put into this treatment. Remind clients to think of progress as an ongoing process that continues after treatment. Strategies to maintain and further improve the application of the skills they have learned are reviewed next.

At this point, administer the questions in Exercise 8.1 to the client. The exercise can be found in the client workbook and also in the appendix at the end of this therapist guide. You and your clients may photocopy this exercise from the workbook or download multiple copies from the website.

If your client endorses significant improvements to items 1 or 2 on Exercise 8.1: My Progress Assessment, congratulate them for their hard work and their success. Then go to the section just below on "Continued Practice."

If your client does not endorse improvement to items 1 or 2, review their answers to items 4 through 12 to identify which specific skill sets may be revisited to achieve further gains.

Continued Practice

An effective way to promote continued practice after treatment is to create a long-term goal list, as shown in Exercise 8.2: My Long-Term Goals. It can be found in the client workbook and also in the appendix at the end of this therapist guide. Encourage the client to think about the following questions:

- *What was this treatment in service of?*
- *Why did you want to improve your mood?*

Writing down the concrete steps creates a sense of structure and accountability. The goal list should include at least one of the skills learned. Examples are "Being a more present parent," "Continue to nurture the relationship with a friend," and "Stay physically active."

Next, use Exercise 8.3: Maintaining My Gains to generate steps to maintain treatment gains through concrete practices in each of the three skills areas: positive activities with savoring the moment, thinking positively, and building positivity. For example, positive activities designed to continue nurturing a friendship may include calling a friend once a week. This exercise can be found in the client workbook and also in the appendix at the end of this therapist guide.

Dealing with Challenging Times and Barriers

Research has shown that continued practice after treatment reduces a client's risk of relapse. The concept of continued practice is best explained by asking a client about skills they have learned in life, such as learning how to walk, bicycle, or drive; learning a new language or sport; or learning how to use a smartphone or computer. Ask your client to imagine what would happen if they stopped practicing after they learned how to drive or use a computer. While the theoretical knowledge can more easily be retained, the practical knowledge decreases over time. Thus, the most crucial time for skill maintenance is early on. Once a skill has been used repeatedly, such as driving, it will become second nature.

Help clients to complete Exercise 8.4: Overcoming Barriers, which can be found in the client workbook and also in the appendix at the end of this therapist guide, to identify the factors that may impede or interrupt effective practice of all of the skills they have learned. Ask the following questions:

- *What do you anticipate getting in the way of you practicing your skills as you move forward?*
- *What do you expect to trip you up?*
- *Which are the more difficult skills for you?*
- *What stressful experiences make it more difficult for you to practice certain skills?*

The combination of anticipating and dealing with future barriers is a powerful tool moving forward. Ask your client to list three barriers on the exercise sheet, and discuss one to three steps they can take to avoid each barrier. Examples include scheduling regular time in their day to practice, setting reminders on their phone, reviewing their workbook once a week or month, and continuing to practice the more difficult skills.

This vignette demonstrates how the therapist handles a client's fear about therapy ending.

C: *I understand that I made some progress, but I feel I am not ready to continue on my own.*

T: *You have certainly shown progress. Can you tell me why you think you are not ready to continue on your own?*

C: *I am worried I will forget how to use the skills I learned.*

T: *I understand your concern. Remember the analogy with learning how to drive?*

C: *Yes, you used it a lot.* (smile)

T: *Yes, indeed! So when you passed your driving test and your instructor sent you off by yourself, did you forget all the skills you had learned?*

C: *Of course not.*

T: *So, what happened instead?*

C: *Well, I just kept driving, and it became easier over time. I started feeling more confident that I knew how to drive a car and what to do in difficult situations.*

T: *So, how does this apply to ending treatment?*

C: *Well, I guess if I continue to apply the skills I learned, the better and more confident I will become.*

T: *Remember that all the skills you learned are described in detail in your workbook. I would encourage you to review them once in a while. You can also review your exercise sheets.*

C: *Do you recommend I continue to fill out the exercise sheets daily?*

T: *This can be a helpful practice for some clients. It depends on what works best for you. You can formally or informally continue the exercises. I would encourage you to test out what works best with your daily practices.*

Troubleshooting

Clients sometimes express concern that they have not improved as much as they had hoped. Some may acknowledge that they have improved but minimize their improvement. As outlined earlier, using objective data from standardized questionnaires (e.g., Positive and Negative Affect

Schedule and Depression, Anxiety and Stress Scales) is an effective way to evaluate their improvement. Emphasize the importance of change relative to baseline severity levels. Discounting progress is common in clients with anhedonia. An exercise in "Attending to the Positive" can be a powerful opportunity to practice its application: that is, the client can generate silver linings of the treatment (*Finding the Silver Linings*), how these silver linings contributed to what they learned (*Taking Ownership*), and how the client can imagine moving forward positively (*Imagining the Positive*). Re-emphasize the concept of continued practice, and that the end of treatment is the beginning of the client's self-guided journey. The analogy of owning a toolbox filled with powerful tools at their disposal is a helpful way to increase confidence, ownership, and positivity.

Some clients are afraid to relapse either because they have suffered multiple prior treatment failures or they mistrust their treatment gains. Whatever the reason for their concern, it is important for you to properly educate clients about the difference between a lapse and a relapse and when to seek additional help.

Start by reminding clients that forming new habits is challenging, especially when the old habits have become automatic. Explain that it is normal to experience moments where they fall back into old habits. Prime times are stressful times. Again, remind clients about other new behaviors they have developed, such as eating healthy or exercising, and how hard it is to keep doing them when buried in deadlines or after recovering from a cold. Explain that those moments are called lapses or slips. They are not a sign of failure or concern, but they should also not be ignored. Advise your clients to be vigilant about lapses (e.g., they stopped their daily walks for a few days because they felt down) and, once recognized, to take the steps forward by continuing to practice skills in a self-compassionate manner. This will ensure that their gains are maintained and will provide them with a sense of control and empowerment.

Lapses are different from relapses. During a lapse, levels of positive or negative mood temporarily fluctuate, but during a relapse, they return to pretreatment levels over days or weeks. Keeping a diary with mood ratings is an effective way to distinguish between lapses and relapses. While regular practice and review of how to deal with barriers can lower the risk of relapses, they can occur, even after a long time of remaining symptom-free. Discuss with your clients whether booster sessions are available. If you do not offer them, provide your client with a referral list of local providers. Emphasize that your client should not delay seeking help, and that sometimes one or two booster sessions can be sufficient to get back on track.

Finally, clients can be fearful or hesitant to continue practicing the skills learned in treatment without being in therapy or working with a therapist. Use the driver's education model for therapy, with the client as the driver and the therapist as the instructor. The therapist initially provides significant support, but with time, the clients lead the therapy by themselves, and the therapist provides less and less support. What would happen if the instructor would continue to go everywhere with the driver once they passed their driver's test? Continued progress after therapy ends is expected, and so are continued challenges. Assure your clients that they are appropriately equipped to deal with most challenges if they keep practicing the skills they have learned.

Client Exercises

This appendix contains a copy of each of the client exercise sheets. These exercises also appear in the client workbook. Therapists and clients may photocopy the exercise sheets from their respective book, or they can download multiple copies at the Treatments That Work[TM] website (www. oxfordclinicalpsych.com/PAT).

Exercise 2.1: Treatment Fit Assessment

	Reward System to Target				Exercise to Practice
	Yes	**Wanting**	**Liking**	**Learning**	
Are you having difficulty feeling positive emotions, like love, joy, curiosity, pride, and excitement?	☐		X		Labeling Emotions
Do you have difficulty noticing the positive in your day to day?	☐		X	X	Finding the Silver Linings
Do you tend to dismiss the positive?	☐		X	X	Gratitude
Do others tell you that you don't give yourself enough credit?	☐		X	X	Taking Ownership
Do you find yourself attributing good things to luck rather than your own doing?	☐		X	X	Taking Ownership
Are you more likely to imagine negative outcomes in the future than positive outcomes?	☐	X		X	Imagining the Positive
Have you stopped engaging in pleasant or enjoyable activities?	☐	X	X	X	Actions Toward Feeling Better
Are you finding it hard to find pleasure in activities you once enjoyed or think you should enjoy?	☐		X	X	Savoring / Generosity
Do you have a hard time getting motivated and excited about activities you once enjoyed or tasks that gave you a sense of accomplishment?	☐	X			Designing Positive Activities
Have you struggled to feel connected with others, including emotions of empathy, love, or compassion?	☐		X	X	Appreciative Joy / Loving-Kindness

Clipart sourced from Microsoft PowerPoint.

Exercise 2.2: Treatment Timing Assessment

	Yes	No
I can commit to completing practice assignments at home nearly every day (at least 3x/week).	☐	☐
I am not engaging in another treatment that will interfere with my ability to engage in this treatment.	☐	☐
I am not experiencing elevations in other symptoms that take priority over this treatment (e.g., suicidality, psychosis, mania, substance abuse).	☐	☐

Exercise 4.1: A Mood Cycle You Noticed

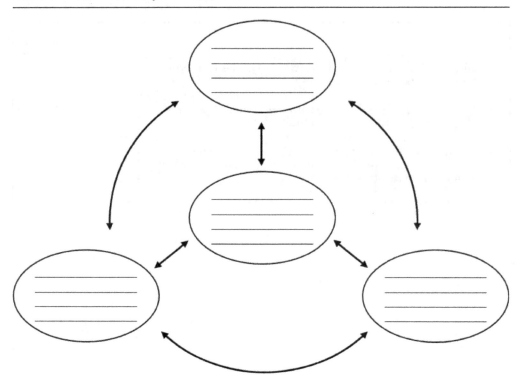

Exercise 4.2: Positive Emotions Dial

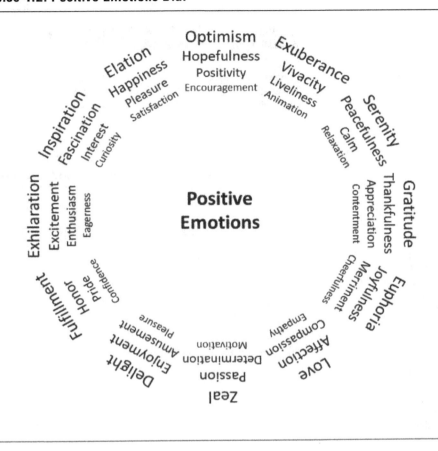

_____

_____

_____

_____

Exercise 5.1: Daily Activity and Mood Record

Daily Activity and Mood Record

Instructions:
Monitor and record your daily activities throughout the day. Be sure to rate your mood before and after each activity (0=lowest mood, 10=highest mood). Try to record your activities every day this week. Use a different Daily Activity and Mood Record for each day.

Day of the Week: _____

	Activity	Mood Before (0-10)	Mood After (0-10)
1.00			
2.00			
3.00			
4.00			
5.00			
6.00			
7.00			
8.00			
9.00			
10.00			
11.00			
12.00			
13.00			
14.00			
15.00			
16.00			
17.00			
18.00			
19.00			
20.00			
21.00			
22.00			
23.00			
24.00			

Exercise 5.2: Positive Activity List

Instructions: Review the list of positive activities. Identify whether each activity is a *current* activity that brings you positive emotions, a *past* activity that brought on positive emotions, or a new activity that you can *try*. Label each positive activity with C for current, P for past, or T for trying something new. Add any additional activities that you currently enjoy, have enjoyed, or think you might enjoy.

C, P, T

_____ Taking a bath

_____ Going to a concert

_____ Going to a sports event

_____ Having lunch with friends or colleagues

_____ Going to bar, tavern, club, etc.

_____ Reading a book for pleasure

_____ Playing with animals

_____ Spending time in nature

_____ Watching a movie, series, or sports

_____ Going to a party

_____ Hanging out with friends

_____ Cooking

_____ Thinking about a positive future

_____ Enjoying a favorite snack

_____ Cuddling with a significant other

_____ Exercising, hiking, or playing sports

_____ Exploring (e.g., going a new route)

_____ Putting on makeup, doing my hair, etc.

_____ Dressing up in nice clothes

_____ Going to the movie theater

_____ Watching funny movies or clips

_____ Getting a massage

_____ _____

_____ _____

C, P, T

_____ Buying things for myself

_____ Going to religious or community functions

_____ Going to class or club event

_____ Buying a gift for family or friends

_____ Donating to charity or volunteering

_____ Making food or crafts to give away

_____ Dancing to my favorite song

_____ Catching up with a friend

_____ Being with children or grandchildren

_____ Helping others

_____ Breathing fresh air

_____ Playing video games with friends

_____ Playing a musical instrument

_____ Doing artwork (e.g., painting, photography)

_____ Smelling my favorite candle scent

_____ Playing cards or board games

_____ Going on a walk

_____ Writing a letter

_____ Looking at pictures

_____ Gardening

_____ Getting a manicure or pedicure

_____ _____

_____ _____

Exercise 5.3: Positive Activity List Through Mastery

Positive Activity List through Mastery

Instructions: Review the list of positive activities that build mastery. Identify whether each activity is a *current* activity that you are practicing, a *past* activity, or a new activity that you can *try*. Label each activity with C for current, P for past, or T for trying something new. Add any additional activities that currently bring on a feeling of mastery or that might bring on that feeling.

C, P, T

_____ Working towards meeting a deadline

_____ Learning a new skill (e.g., language)

_____ Finishing a project

_____ Cleaning the dishes

_____ Vacuuming

_____ Organizing

_____ Planning trips or vacations

_____ Studying for an exam

_____ Working on a jigsaw puzzle

_____ _____

_____ _____

C, P, T

_____ Learning a musical instrument

_____ Reading a book

_____ Writing stories, novels, plays, or poetry

_____ Learning a new hobby (e.g., craft)

_____ Redecorating a room

_____ Working on an application

_____ Restoring furniture or antiques

_____ Arranging songs or music

_____ Completing homework

_____ _____

_____ _____

Exercise 5.4: My Positive Activity List

My Positive Activity List

Record: (1) activities that you currently find enjoyable, once found enjoyable, or believe that you could find enjoyable, (2) activities that bring value to your life, and (3) activities that may not bring immediate enjoyment but produce feelings of mastery (or other positive emotions) following their completion. Rate the level of difficulty (0 – easy, 10 – most difficult) for you to complete each item.

Activity	Difficulty (0–10)
1. _____	_____
2. _____	_____
3. _____	_____
4. _____	_____
5. _____	_____
6. _____	_____
7. _____	_____
8. _____	_____
9. _____	_____
10. _____	_____

Exercise 5.5: Positive Activity Scheduling

Positive Activity Scheduling

Instructions:

Identify one new activity from your Positive Activity List that you can engage in this week. Write this activity in the Activity box. Identify which category (e.g., social, work, health, leisure, spirituality, other) the activity falls into. If your activity requires steps to complete it, enter those steps in the How to Complete Activity box. Rate the difficulty level of each step on a 0-10 scale (0=least difficult, 10=most difficult). Then complete the paragraph, filling in the number of times in the week, the days in the week, time of day, the duration, and who you might be doing the activity with. Then, practice the activity throughout the week, recording your mood before and after on a 0-10 scale (0=lowest mood, 10=highest mood). Also, record any positive emotions you may have noticed before, during, or after engaging in the activity.

Activity

Category
☐ Social ☐ Leisure ☐ Work ☐ Spirituality ☐ Health ☐ Other

How to Complete Activity

Steps	Difficulty (0-10)
1. _____	_____
2. _____	_____
3. _____	_____
4. _____	_____
5. _____	_____
6. _____	_____
7. _____	_____
8. _____	_____

For homework, I will complete this activity _____ times this week, on _____ (M, Tu, W, etc.) in the _____ (morning, afternoon, evening) for _____ (# of: sec, min, hrs) with _____(name; if applicable).

Homework #	Mood Before (0-10)	Mood After (0-10)	Positive Emotion(s)
1			
2			
3			
4			
5			
6			
7			

Exercise 5.6: Savoring the Moment

Savoring the Moment

Instructions: Identify and record a positive activity or event from this week. Recount the event in your mind, Visualizing what you saw, heard, felt, thought, smelled, and tasted. Record your level of mood (0=lowest mood, 10=highest mood) before and after the recounting, as well as the vividness of the recounting (10=most vivid). Also, identify any positive emotions you noticed, in addition to any other reactions (e.g., thoughts, physical sensations).

Event	Mood Before (0-10)	Mood After (0-10)	Vividness (0-10)	Positive Emotion(s)	Reactions (thoughts, physical sensations)

Exercise 6.1: Finding the Silver Linings

Finding the Silver Linings

Instructions: Record the date of your practice. Then identify and record a positive, negative, or neutral situation. Identify as many positive aspects (at least 6) of that situation, and write them down under Silver Linings. Don't forget to write down your mood before and after the exercise on a 0-10 scale (0=lowest mood, 10=highest mood). Also, write down any positive emotions you experienced before, during, or after the exercise. Try to complete one exercise a day.

Practice Date: _____

Situation: _____

_____

_____

Silver Linings:

1 _____

2. _____

3. _____

4. _____

5. _____

6. _____

Mood Before (0-10)	**Mood After (0-10)**	**Positive Emotion(s)**
_____	_____	_____

Exercise 6.2: Taking Ownership

Taking Ownership

Instructions: Record the date of your practice. Then identify and record a positive situation. Identify as many positive aspects (at least 6) of that situation, and write them down under Contributions. Don't forget to write down your mood before and after the exercise on a 0-10 scale (0=lowest mood, 10=highest mood). Also, write down any positive emotions you experienced before, during, or after the exercise. Try to complete one exercise a day.

Practice Date: _____

Situation: _____

_____

_____

Contributions:

1. _____

2. _____

3. _____

4. _____

5. _____

6. _____

Mood Before (0-10)	**Mood After (0-10)**	**Positive Emotion(s)**
_____	_____	_____

Exercise 6.3: Imagining the Positive

Imagining the Positive

Instructions: Identify a possible future event. Describe the future event with the best possible outcome. Write it as if it were happening right now (present tense), using details of your emotions, thoughts, and physical sensation (e.g., sight, smell, hearing).

- -

Now imagine this vividly. Don't forget to write down your mood before and after the exercise on a 0-10 scale (0=lowest mood, 10=highest mood), as well as the vividness of the recounting (10=most vivid). Also, write down any positive emotions you experienced before, during, or after the exercise. Try to complete one per day.

Mood Before (0-10)	Mood After(0-10)	Vividness (0-10)	Positive Emotion(s)

Exercise 7.1: Loving-Kindness

Loving-Kindness

Instructions: Record the date of your practice. Identify at least one recipient of your *Loving-Kindness* practice. It can be helpful to start with someone uncomplicated. Read or listen to the *Loving-Kindness* script or recording. Be sure to record your mood (0= lowest mood, 10=highest mood) before and after your practice, as well as any positive emotions, thoughts, or physical sensations you notice. Try to complete one per day.

Practice Date: _____

Recipient(s) of Practice: _____

Mood Before (0-10): _____

Mood After (0-10): _____

Positive Emotion(s): _____

_____

Reaction (thoughts, physical sensations):

_____

_____

_____

_____

Exercise 7.2: Gratitude

Gratitude

Instructions: Record the date of your practice. List 5 things you notice and appreciate each day, making sure that they are different from the previous day. Record your mood (0=lowest mood, 10=highest mood) before and after making the list. Also, write down any positive emotions you notice. Try to complete one exercise per day.

Date: _____

Today I am grateful for...

1. _____

2. _____

3. _____

4. _____

5. _____

Mood Before (0-10): _____

Mood After (0-10): _____

Positive Emotion(s): _____

_____

Exercise 7.3: Generosity

Generosity

Instructions: Record the date and time of your generous act. Identify and record what your generous act will be and who will be the recipient of it. Record your mood (0= lowest mood, 10=highest mood) before and after doing the generous act. Also, write down any positive emotions you notice. Try to complete 3 per week.

Date/Time: _____

Act: _____

Recipient: _____

Mood Before (0-10): _____

Mood After (0-10): _____

Positive Emotion(s): _____

_____

Exercise 7.4: Appreciative Joy

Appreciative Joy

Instructions: Record the date of your practice. Identify at least one recipient of your *Appreciative Joy* practice. It can be helpful to start with someone uncomplicated. Read or listen to the *Appreciative Joy* script or recording. Be sure to record your mood (0= lowest mood, 10=highest mood) before and after your practice, as well as any positive emotions, thoughts, or physical sensations you notice. Try to complete one practice per day.

Practice Date: _____

Recipient(s) of Practice: _____

Mood Before (0-10): _____

Mood After (0-10): _____

Positive Emotion(s): _____

Reaction (thoughts, physical sensations):

_____

_____

_____

_____

Exercise 8.1: My Progress Assessment

Overall Treatment Evaluation: Positive Mood

1. Has your overall mood improved since the start of treatment?
2. Are you feeling positive emotions more *frequently*? Are you noticing *more* positive emotions throughout your day or week? Do you feel certain positive emotions *more intensely*?

Overall Treatment Evaluation: Negative Mood

3. What about your negative mood?

Treatment Evaluation: Core Components

Chapter 5: Actions Toward Feeling Better

4. Are you engaging in more meaningful activities? Are you able to savor the activities that you already engage in?
5. Have you been incorporating more positive activities throughout your day and week?

Chapter 6: Attending to the Positive

6. Are you noticing silver linings every day?
7. Are you giving yourself credit for things you did well? Are you accepting praise without dismissing it? Are you attributing some positive events to your own doing?
8. Are you taking time to imagine future events positively?

Chapter 7: Building Positivity

9. Are you having more loving and kind feelings toward yourself and others?
10. Are you noticing feeling joy from the successes and joy of others?
11. Are you feeling more grateful each day, even during times of stress?
12. Are you more generous to others or yourself? Have you been engaging in even tiny acts of generosity (e.g., kindness, helping hand, a listening ear, advice) a few times a week?

Exercise 8.2: My Long-Term Goals

My Long-Term Goals

Instructions: Identify at least 1-3 goals that you have for after treatment. What was this treatment in service of? Why did you want to improve your mood? Identify any steps that you need to take to meet each goal. Identify one of the skills from this treatment as a step towards meeting one of your goals.

My long-term goals are...

1. _____

    Step 1. _____

    Step 2. _____

    Step 3. _____

2. _____

    Step 1. _____

    Step 2. _____

    Step 3. _____

3. _____

    Step 1. _____

    Step 2. _____

    Step 3. _____

Exercise 8.3: Maintaining My Gains

Maintaining My Gains

Instructions: Answer each of these questions. Identify how you will maintain your gains in treatment through skills from Actions Toward Feeling Better, Attending to the Positive, and Building Positivity.

How will I maintain my gains through *Actions Toward Feeling Better*?

1._____

2._____

3._____

How will I maintain my gains through *Attending to the Positive*?

1._____

2._____

3._____

How will I maintain my gains through *Building Positivity*?

1._____

2._____

3._____

Exercise 8.4: Overcoming Barriers

Overcoming Barriers

Instructions: Identify possible barriers that might interfere with you meeting one of your long-term goals. List 1-3 steps you can take to avoid that barrier.

Barriers...

1. _____

    Step 1. _____

    Step 2. _____

    Step 3. _____

2. _____

    Step 1. _____

    Step 2. _____

    Step 3. _____

3. _____

    Step 1. _____

    Step 2. _____

    Step 3. _____

Recommended Readings

Auerbach, R. P., Pagliaccio, D., & Pizzagalli, D. A. (2019) Toward an improved understanding of anhedonia. *JAMA Psychiatry, 76*(6), 571–573.

Craske, M. G., Meuret, A., Ritz, T., Treanor, M., & Dour, H. (2016). Treatment for anhedonia: A neuroscience-driven approach. *Depression and Anxiety, 33*(10), 927–938.

Craske, M. G., Meuret, A., Ritz, T., Treanor, M., Dour, H., & Rosenfield, D. (2019). Positive affect treatment for depression and anxiety: A randomized clinical trial for a core feature of anhedonia. *Journal of Consulting and Clinical Psychology, 87*(5), 457–471.

Vinograd, M., & Craske, M. G. (2020). Using neuroscience to augment behavioral interventions for depression. *Harvard Review of Psychiatry, 28*(1), 14–25.

References

Aknin, L. B., Broesch, T., Hamlin, J. K., & Van de Vondervoort, J. W. (2015). Prosocial behavior leads to happiness in a small-scale rural society. *Journal of Experimental Psychology, General, 144*(4), 788–795. https://doi.org/10.1037/xge0000082

Algoe, S. B., & Haidt, J. (2009). Witnessing excellence in action: The "other-praising" emotions of elevation, gratitude, and admiration. *Journal of Positive Psychology, 4*(2), 105–127. https://doi.org/10.1080/17439760802650519

American Psychiatric Association. (2016). *Diagnostic and statistical manual of mental disorders* (5th ed.). American Psychiatric Publishing. https://doi.org/10.1016/B978-0-12-809324-5.05530-9

Ballard, E. D., Wills, K., Lally, N., Richards, E. M., Luckenbaugh, D. A., Walls, T., Ameli, R., Niciu, M. J., Brutsche, N. E., Park, L., & Zarate, C. A. (2017). Anhedonia as a clinical correlate of suicidal thoughts in clinical ketamine trials. *Journal of Affective Disorders, 218*, 195–200. https://doi.org/10.1016/j.jad.2017.04.057

Barry, T. J., Sze, W. Y., & Raes, F. (2019). A meta-analysis and systematic review of Memory Specificity Training (MeST) in the treatment of emotional disorders. *Behaviour Research and Therapy, 116*, 36–51. https://doi.org/10.1016/j.brat.2019.02.001

Bénabou, R., & Tirole, J. (2006). Incentives and prosocial behavior. *American Economic Review, 96*(5), 1652–1678. https://doi.org/10.1257/aer.96.5.1652

Berridge, K. C., & Kringelbach, M. L. (2015). Pleasure systems in the brain. *Neuron, 86*(3), 646–664. https://doi.org/10.1016/j.neuron.2015.02.018

Borgonovi, F. (2008). Doing well by doing good: The relationship between formal volunteering and self-reported health and happiness. *Social Science & Medicine, 66*(11), 2321–2334. https://doi.org/10.1016/j.socscimed.2008.01.011

Boumparis, N., Karyotaki, E., Kleiboer, A., Hofmann, S. G., & Cuijpers, P. (2016). The effect of psychotherapeutic interventions on positive and negative affect in depression: A systematic review and meta-analysis.

Journal of Affective Disorders, 202, 153–162. https://doi.org/10.1016/
j.jad.2016.05.019

Brewin, C. R. (2006). Understanding cognitive behaviour therapy: A re-
trieval competition account. *Behaviour Research and Therapy, 44*(6),
765–784. https://doi.org/10.1016/j.brat.2006.02.005

Brown, T. A., & Barlow, D. H. (2021). *Anxiety and Related Disorders
Interview Schedule for DSM-5 (ADIS-5)—Adult Version Client Interview
Schedule 5-Copy Set.* Oxford University Press.

Brown, T. A., Chorpita, B. F., & Barlow, D. H. (1998). Structural
relationships among dimensions of the DSM-IV anxiety and mood
disorders and dimensions of negative affect, positive affect, and auto-
nomic arousal. *Journal of Abnormal Psychology, 107*(2), 179–192.

Carson, J. W., Keefe, F. J., Lynch, T. R., Carson, K. M., Goli, V., Fras, A.
M., & Thorp, S. R. (2005). Loving-kindness meditation for chronic
low back pain: Results from a pilot trial. *Journal of Holistic Nursing,
23*(3), 287–304. https://doi.org/10.1177/0898010105277651

Christov-Moore, L., Sugiyama, T., Grigaityte, K., & Iacoboni, M. (2017).
Increasing generosity by disrupting prefrontal cortex. *Social Neuroscience,
12*(2), 174–181. https://doi.org/10.1080/17470919.2016.1154105

Chung, Y. S., & Barch, D. (2015). Anhedonia is associated with reduced
incentive cue related activation in the basal ganglia. *Cognitive, Affective
and Behavioral Neuroscience, 15*(4), 749–767. https://doi.org/10.3758/
s13415-015-0366-3

Clark, L. A., & Watson, D. (1991). Tripartite model of anxiety and
depression: Psychometric evidence and taxonomic implications. *Journal
of Abnormal Psychology, 100*(3), 316–336. https://doi.org/10.1037//
0021-843x.100.3.316

Clepce, M., Gossler, A., Reich, K., Kornhuber, J., & Thuerauf, N. (2010).
The relation between depression, anhedonia and olfactory hedonic
estimates: A pilot study in major depression. *Neuroscience Letters,
471*(3), 139–143. https://doi.org/10.1016/j.neulet.2010.01.027

Craske, M. G., Meuret, A. E., Ritz, T., Treanor, M., & Dour, H. J. (2016).
Treatment for anhedonia: A neuroscience driven approach. *Depression
and Anxiety, 33*(10), 927–938. https://doi.org/10.1002/da.22490

Craske, M. G., Meuret, A., Ritz, T., Treanor, M., Dour, H., & Rosenfield,
D. (2019). Positive Affect Treatment for Depression and Anxiety: A
randomized clinical trial for a core feature of anhedonia. *Journal of
Consulting and Clinical Psychology, 87*(5), 457–471. https://doi.org/
10.1037/ccp0000396

Demyttenaere, K., Donneau, A. F., Albert, A., Ansseau, M., Constant,
E., & Van Heeringen, K. (2015). What is important in being cured

from depression? Discordance between physicians and patients. *Journal of Affective Disorders, 174*, 390–396. https://doi.org/10.1016/j.jad.2014.12.004

Der-Avakian, A., & Markou, A. (2012). The neurobiology of anhedonia and other reward-related deficits. *Trends in Neurosciences, 35*(1), 68–77. https://doi.org/10.1016/j.tins.2011.11.005

DeRubeis, R. J., Hollon, S. D., Amsterdam, J. D., Shelton, R. C., Young, P. R., Salomon, R. M., O'Reardon, J. P., Lovett, M. L., Gladis, M. M., Brown, L. L., & Gallop, R. (2005). Cognitive therapy vs. medications in the treatment of moderate to severe depression. *Archives of General Psychiatry, 62*(4), 409–416. https://doi.org/10.1001/archpsyc.62.4.409

DeShea, L. (2003). A scenario-based scale of Willingness to Forgive. *Individual Differences Research, 1*(3), 201–216.Dichter, G. S., Felder, J. N., Petty, C., Bizzell, J., Ernst, M., & Smoski, M. J. (2009). The effects of psychotherapy on neural responses to rewards in major depression. *Biological Psychiatry, 66*(9), 886–897. https://doi.org/10.1016/j.biopsych.2009.06.021

Dimidjian, S., Hollon, S. D., Dobson, K. S., Schmaling, K. B., Kohlenberg, R. J., Addis, M. E., Gallop, R., McGlinchey, J. B., Markley, D. K., Gollan, J. K., Atkins, D. C., Dunner, D. L., & Jacobson, N. S. (2006). Randomized trial of behavioral activation, cognitive therapy, and antidepressant medication in the acute treatment of adults with major depression. *Journal of Consulting and Clinical Psychology, 74*(4), 658–670. https://doi.org/10.1037/0022-006X.74.4.658

Dobson, K. S., Hollon, S. D., Dimidjian, S., Schmaling, K. B., Kohlenberg, R. J., Gallop, R. J., Rizvi, S. L., Gollan, J. K., Dunner, D. L., & Jacobson, N. S. (2008). Randomized trial of behavioral activation, cognitive therapy, and antidepressant medication in the prevention of relapse and recurrence in major depression. *Journal of Consulting and Clinical Psychology, 76*(3), 468–477. https://doi.org/10.1037/0022-006X.76.3.468

Ducasse, D., Dubois, J., Jaussent, I., Azorin, J. M., Etain, B., Gard, S., Henry, C., Bougerol, T., Kahn, J. P., Aubin, V., Bellivier, F., Belzeaux, R., Dubertret, C., Dubreucq, J., Llorca, P. M., Loftus, J., Passerieux, C., Polosan, M., Samalin, L., . . . Courtet, P. (2021). Association between anhedonia and suicidal events in patients with mood disorders: A 3-year prospective study. *Depression and Anxiety, 38*, 17–27. https://doi.org/10.1002/da.23072

Ducasse, D., Loas, G., Dassa, D., Gramaglia, C., Zeppegno, P., Guillaume, S., Olié, E., & Courtet, P. (2018). Anhedonia is associated with suicidal ideation independently of depression: A meta-analysis. *Depression and Anxiety, 35*(5), 382–392. https://doi.org/10.1002/da.22709

Dunn, B. D. (2012). Helping depressed clients reconnect to positive emotion experience: Current insights and future directions. *Clinical Psychology and Psychotherapy, 19*(4), 326–340. https://doi.org/10.1002/cpp.1799

Dunn, E. W., Aknin, L. B., & Norton, M. I. (2008). Spending money on others promotes happiness. *Science, 319*(5870), 1687–1688. https://doi.org/10.1126/science.1150952

Emmons, R. A., & McCullough, M. E. (2003). Counting blessings versus burdens: An experimental investigation of gratitude and subjective well-being in daily life. *Journal of Personality and Social Psychology, 84*(2), 377–389. https://doi.org/10.1037//0022-3514.84.2.377

Fawcett, J., Scheftner, W. A., Fogg, L., Clark, D. C., Young, M. A., Hedeker, D., & Gibbons, R. (1990). Time-related predictors of suicide in major affective disorder. *American Journal of Psychiatry, 147*(9), 1189–1194. https://doi.org/10.1176/ajp.147.9.1189

Fiorito, E. R., & Simons, R. F. (1994). Emotional imagery and physical anhedonia. *Psychophysiology, 31*(5), 513–521. https://doi.org/10.1111/j.1469-8986.1994.tb01055.x

First, M. B., Williams, J. B. W., Karg, R. S., & Spitzer, R. L. (2016). *Structured Clinical Interview for DSM-5 Disorders, Clinician Version (SCID-5-CV)*. American Psychiatric Association.

Fitzgibbons, L., & Simons, R. F. (1992). Affective response to color-slide stimuli in subjects with physical anhedonia: A three-systems analysis. *Psychophysiology, 29*(6), 613–620. https://doi.org/10.1111/j.1469-8986.1992.tb02036.x

Forbes, C. N. (2020). New directions in behavioral activation: Using findings from basic science and translational neuroscience to inform the exploration of potential mechanisms of change. *Clinical Psychology Review, 79*, 101860. https://doi.org/10.1016/j.cpr.2020.101860

Fox, G. R., Kaplan, J., Damasio, H., & Damasio, A. (2015). Neural correlates of gratitude. *Frontiers in Psychology, 6.* Article 1491. doi:10.3389/fpsyg.2015.01491

Fredrickson, B. L. (2001). The role of positive emotions in positive psychology: The broaden-and-build theory of positive emotions. *American Psychologist, 56*(3), 218–226. https://doi.org/10.1037//0003-066x.56.3.218

Fredrickson, B. L., Cohn, M. A., Coffey, K. A., Pek, J., & Finkel, S. M. (2008). Open hearts build lives: Positive emotions, induced through loving-kindness meditation, build consequential personal resources.

Journal of Personality and Social Psychology, 95(5), 1045–1062. https://doi.org/10.1037/a0013262

Fredrickson, B. L., & Joiner, T. (2002). Positive emotions trigger upward spirals toward emotional well-being. *Psychological Science, 13*(2), 172–175. https://doi.org/10.1111/1467-9280.00431

Froh, J. J., Kashdan, T. B., Ozimkowski, K. M., & Miller, N. (2009). Who benefits the most from a gratitude intervention in children and adolescents? Examining positive affect as a moderator. *Journal of Positive Psychology, 4*(5), 408–422. https://doi.org/10.1080/17439760902992464

Gard, D. E., Gard, M. G., Kring, A. M., & John, O. P. (2006). Anticipatory and consummatory components of the experience of pleasure: A scale development study. *Journal of Research in Personality, 40*(6), 1086–1102. https://doi.org/10.1016/j.jrp.2005.11.001

Garland, E. L., Fredrickson, B., Kring, A. M., Johnson, D. P., Meyer, P. S., & Penn, D. L. (2010). Upward spirals of positive emotions counter downward spirals of negativity: Insights from the broaden-and-build theory and affective neuroscience on the treatment of emotion dysfunctions and deficits in psychopathology. *Clinical Psychology Review, 30*(7), 849–864. https://doi.org/10.1016/j.cpr.2010.03.002

Geraghty, A. W. A., Wood, A. M., & Hyland, M. E. (2010a). Dissociating the facets of hope: Agency and pathways predict dropout from unguided self-help therapy in opposite directions. *Journal of Research in Personality, 44*(1), 155–158. https://doi.org/https://doi.org/10.1016/j.jrp.2009.12.003

Geraghty, A. W. A., Wood, A. M., & Hyland, M. E. (2010b). Attrition from self-directed interventions: Investigating the relationship between psychological predictors, intervention content and dropout from a body dissatisfaction intervention. *Social Science & Medicine, 71*(1), 30–37. https://doi.org/10.1016/j.socscimed.2010.03.007

Gradin, V. B., Kumar, P., Waiter, G., Ahearn, T., Stickle, C., Milders, M., Reid, I., Hall, J., & Steele, J. D. (2011). Expected value and prediction error abnormalities in depression and schizophrenia. *Brain, 134*(6), 1751–1764. https://doi.org/10.1093/brain/awr059

Greenberg, T., Chase, H. W., Almeida, J. R., Stiffler, R., Zevallos, C. R., Aslam, H. A., Deckersbach, T., Weyandt, S., Cooper, C., Toups, M., Carmody, T., Kurian, B., Peltier, S., Adams, P., McInnis, M. G., Oquendo, M. A., McGrath, P. J., Fava, M., Weissman, M., . . . Phillips, M. L. (2015). Moderation of the relationship between reward expectancy and prediction error-related ventral striatal reactivity by anhedonia in unmedicated major depressive disorder: Findings from the

EMBARC study. *American Journal of Psychiatry, 172*(9), 881–891. https://doi.org/10.1176/appi.ajp.2015.14050594

Gross, J. J. (1998). The emerging field of emotion regulation: An integrative review. *Review of General Psychology, 2*(3), 271–299. https://doi.org/10.1037/1089-2680.2.3.271

Grossman, P. (2015). Mindfulness: Awareness informed by an embodied ethic. *Mindfulness, 6*(1), 17–22. https://doi.org/10.1007/s12671-014-0372-5

Hallford, D. J., Farrell, H., & Lynch, E. (2020a). Increasing anticipated and anticipatory pleasure through episodic thinking. *Emotion.* https://doi.org/10.1037/emo0000765

Hallford, D. J., Sharma, M. K., & Austin, D. W. (2020b). Increasing anticipatory pleasure in major depression through enhancing episodic future thinking: A randomized single-case series trial. *Journal of Psychopathology and Behavioral Assessment, 42,* 751–764. https://doi.org/10.1007/s10862-020-09820-9

Hamilton, W. D. (1963). The evolution of altruistic behavior. *American Naturalist, 97,* 354–356. https://doi.org/10.1086/497114

Hofmann, S. G., Grossman, P., & Hinton, D. E. (2011). Loving-kindness and compassion meditation: Potential for psychological interventions. *Clinical Psychology Review, 31*(7), 1126–1132. https://doi.org/10.1016/j.cpr.2011.07.003

Hofmann, S. G., Petrocchi, N., Steinberg, J., Lin, M., Arimitsu, K., Kind, S., Mendes, A., & Stangier, U. (2015). Loving-kindness meditation to target affect in mood disorders: A proof-of-concept study. *Evidence-Based Complementary and Alternative Medicine, 2015,* 269126. https://doi.org/10.1155/2015/269126

Holmes, D., Murray, S. J., Perron, A., & Rail, G. (2006). Deconstructing the evidence-based discourse in health sciences: Truth, power and fascism. *International Journal of Evidence-Based Healthcare, 4*(3), 180–186. https://doi.org/10.1111/j.1479-6988.2006.00041.x

Holmes, E. A., Blackwell, S. E., Burnett Heyes, S., Renner, F., & Raes, F. (2016). Mental imagery in depression: Phenomenology, potential mechanisms, and treatment implications. *Annual Review of Clinical Psychology, 12*(1), 249–280. https://doi.org/10.1146/annurev-clinpsy-021815-092925

Holmes, E. A., Coughtrey, A. E., & Connor, A. (2008a). Looking at or through rose-tinted glasses? Imagery perspective and positive mood. *Emotion, 8*(6), 875–879. https://doi.org/10.1037/a0013617

Holmes, E. A., Mathews, A., Mackintosh, B., & Dalgleish, T. (2008b). The causal effect of mental imagery on emotion assessed using picture-word cues. *Emotion, 8*(3), 395–409. https://doi.org/10.1037/1528-3542.8.3.395

Honkalampi, K., Hintikka, J., Laukkanen, E., Lehtonen, J., & Viinamäki, H. (2001). Alexithymia and depression: A prospective study of patients with major depressive disorder. *Psychosomatics, 42*(3), 229–234. https://doi.org/10.1176/appi.psy.42.3.229

Hopper, J. W., Pitman, R. K., Su, Z., Heyman, G. M., Lasko, N. B., Macklin, M. L., Orr, S. P., Lukas, S. E., & Elman, I. (2008). Probing reward function in posttraumatic stress disorder: Expectancy and satisfaction with monetary gains and losses. *Journal of Psychiatric Research, 42*(10), 802–807. https://doi.org/10.1016/j.jpsychires.2007.10.008

Hutcherson, C. A., Seppala, E. M., & Gross, J. J. (2008). Loving-kindness meditation increases social connectedness. *Emotion, 8*(5), 720–724. https://doi.org/10.1037/a0013237

Johnson, D. P., Penn, D. L., Fredrickson, B. L., Meyer, P. S., Kring, A. M., & Brantley, M. (2009). Loving-kindness meditation to enhance recovery from negative symptoms of schizophrenia. *Journal of Clinical Psychology, 65*(5), 499–509. https://doi.org/10.1002/jclp.20591

Kashdan, T. B., Weeks, J. W., & Savostyanova, A. A. (2011). Whether, how, and when social anxiety shapes positive experiences and events: A self-regulatory framework and treatment implications. *Clinical Psychology Review, 31*(5), 786–799. https://doi.org/10.1016/j.cpr.2011.03.012

Kearney, D. J., Malte, C. A., McManus, C., Martinez, M. E., Felleman, B., & Simpson, T. L. (2013). Loving-kindness meditation for posttraumatic stress disorder: A pilot study. *Journal of Traumatic Stress, 26*(4), 426–434. https://doi.org/10.1002/jts.21832

Kendall, A. D., Zinbarg, R. E., Mineka, S., Bobova, L., Prenoveau, J. M., Revelle, W., & Craske, M. G. (2015). Prospective associations of low positive emotionality with first onsets of depressive and anxiety disorders: Results from a 10-wave latent trait-state modeling study. *Journal of Abnormal Psychology, 124*(4), 933–943. https://doi.org/10.1037/abn0000105

Kessler, R. C., Chiu, W. T., Demler, O., Merikangas, K. R., & Walters, E. E. (2005). Prevalence, severity, and comorbidity of 12-month DSM-IV disorders in the National Comorbidity Survey Replication. *Archives of General Psychiatry, 62*(6), 617–627. https://doi.org/10.1001/archpsyc.62.6.617

Khazanov, G. K., & Ruscio, A. M. (2016). Is low positive emotionality a specific risk factor for depression? A meta-analysis of longitudinal studies. *Psychological Bulletin, 142*(9), 991–1015. https://doi.org/10.1037/bul0000059

Kirkpatrick, M., Delton, A. W., Robertson, T. E., & de Wit, H. (2015). Prosocial effects of MDMA: A measure of generosity. *Journal of Psychopharmacology*, *29*(6), 661–668. https://doi.org/10.1177/0269881115573806

Koole, S. L., Smeets, K., van Knippenberg, A., & Dijksterhuis, A. (1999). The cessation of rumination through self-affirmation. *Journal of Personality and Social Psychology*, *77*(1), 111–125. https://doi.org/10.1037/0022-3514.77.1.111

Koster, E. H. W., De Raedt, R., Goeleven, E., Franck, E., & Crombez, G. (2005). Mood-congruent attentional bias in dysphoria: Maintained attention to and impaired disengagement from negative information. *Emotion*, *5*(4), 446–455. https://doi.org/10.1037/1528-3542.5.4.446

Kotov, R., Gamez, W., Schmidt, F., & Watson, D. (2010). Linking "big" personality traits to anxiety, depressive, and substance use disorders: A meta-analysis. *Psychological Bulletin*, *136*(5), 768–821. https://doi.org/10.1037/a0020327

Landén, M., Högberg, P., & Thase, M. E. (2005). Incidence of sexual side effects in refractory depression during treatment with citalopram or paroxetine. *Journal of Clinical Psychiatry*, *66*(1), 100–106. https://doi.org/10.4088/JCP.v66n0114

Lang, P. J., & Bradley, M. M. (2013). Appetitive and defensive motivation: Goal-directed or Goal-determined? *Emotion Review*, *5*(3), 230–234. https://doi.org/10.1177/1754073913477511

Lang, P. J., & Davis, M. (2006). Emotion, motivation, and the brain: Reflex foundations in animal and human research. Progress in Brain Research, *156*, 3–29. https://doi.org/https://doi.org/10.1016/S0079-6123(06)56001-7

Layous, K., Chancellor, J., & Lyubomirsky, S. (2014). Positive activities as protective factors against mental health conditions. *Journal of Abnormal Psychology*, *123*(1), 3–12. https://doi.org/10.1037/a0034709

Lewinsohn, P. M. (1974). A behavioral approach to depression. In R. Friedman & M. Katz (Eds.), *The psychology of depression: Contemporary theory and research* (pp. 157–185). Wiley.

Lewinsohn, P. M., & Libet, J. (1972). Pleasant events, activity schedules, and depressions. *Journal of Abnormal Psychology*, *79*(3), 291–295. https://doi.org/10.1037/h0033207

Litz, B. T., Orsillo, S. M., Kaloupek, D., & Weathers, F. (2000). Emotional processing in posttraumatic stress disorder. *Journal of Abnormal Psychology*, *109*(1), 26–39. https://doi.org/10.1037/0021-843X.109.1.26

Lovibond, P. F., & Lovibond, S. H. (1995). The structure of negative emotional states: Comparison of the Depression Anxiety Stress Scales (DASS) with the Beck Depression and Anxiety Inventories. *Behaviour Research and Therapy*, *33*(3), 335–343. https://doi.org/10.1016/0005-7967(94)00075-u

MacLeod, A. K., Rose, G. S., & Williams, J. M. (1993). Components of hopelessness about the future in parasuicide. *Cognitive Therapy and Research*, *17*(5), 441–455. https://doi.org/10.1007/BF01173056

Mahler, S. V., Smith, K. S., & Berridge, K. C. (2007). Endocannabinoid hedonic hotspot for sensory pleasure: Anandamide in nucleus accumbens shell enhances "liking" of a sweet reward. *Neuropsychopharmacology*, *32*(11), 2267–2278. https://doi.org/10.1038/sj.npp.1301376

Maltby, J., Wood, A. M., Day, L., Kon, T. W. H., Colley, A., & Linley, P. A. (2008). Personality predictors of levels of forgiveness two and a half years after the transgression. *Journal of Research in Personality*, *42*(4), 1088–1094. https://doi.org/https://doi.org/10.1016/j.jrp.2007.12.008

Martell, C., Dimidjian, S., & Herman-Dunn, R. (2010). *Behavioral activation for depression: A clinician's guide*. Guilford.

Mayhew, S. L., & Gilbert, P. (2008). Compassionate mind training with people who hear malevolent voices: A case series report. *Clinical Psychology & Psychotherapy*, *15*(2), 113–138. https://doi.org/10.1002/cpp.566

McCabe, C., Mishor, Z., Cowen, P. J., & Harmer, C. J. (2010). Diminished neural processing of aversive and rewarding stimuli during selective serotonin reuptake inhibitor treatment. *Biological Psychiatry*, *67*(5), 439–445. https://doi.org/10.1016/j.biopsych.2009.11.001

McCullough, M. E., Emmons, R. A., & Tsang, J.-A. (2002). The grateful disposition: A conceptual and empirical topography. *Journal of Personality and Social Psychology*, *82*(1), 112–127. https://doi.org/10.1037//0022-3514.82.1.112

McFarland, B. R., & Klein, D. N. (2009). Emotional reactivity in depression: Diminished responsiveness to anticipated reward but not to anticipated punishment or to nonreward or avoidance. *Depression and Anxiety*, *26*(2), 117–122. https://doi.org/10.1002/da.20513

Mcisaac, H. K., & Eich, E. (2002). Vantage point in episodic memory. *Psychonomic Bulletin and Review*, *9*(1), 146–150. https://doi.org/10.3758/BF03196271

McMakin, D. L., Siegle, G. J., & Shirk, S. R. (2011). Positive Affect Stimulation and Sustainment (PASS) module for depressed mood: A preliminary investigation of treatment-related effects. *Cognitive Therapy and Research*, *35*(3), 217–226. https://doi.org/10.1007/s10608-010-9311-5

Moore, R. C., Chattillion, E. A., Ceglowski, J., Ho, J., von Känel, R., Mills, P. J., Ziegler, M. G., Patterson, T. L., Grant, I., & Mausbach, B. T. (2013). A randomized clinical trial of Behavioral Activation (BA) therapy for improving psychological and physical health in dementia caregivers: Results of the Pleasant Events Program (PEP). *Behaviour Research and Therapy*, *51*(10), 623–632. https://doi.org/10.1016/j.brat.2013.07.005

Morris, B. H., Bylsma, L. M., & Rottenberg, J. (2009). Does emotion predict the course of major depressive disorder? A review of prospective studies. *British Journal of Clinical Psychology*, *48*(3), 255–273. https://doi.org/10.1348/014466508X396549

Morris, B. H., Bylsma, L. M., Yaroslavsky, I., Kovacs, M., & Rottenberg, J. (2015). Reward learning in pediatric depression and anxiety: Preliminary findings in a high-risk sample. *Depression and Anxiety*, *32*(5), 373–381. https://doi.org/10.1002/da.22358

Mundt, J. C., Marks, I. M., Shear, M. K., & Greist, J. H. (2002). The Work and Social Adjustment Scale: A simple measure of impairment in functioning. *British Journal of Psychiatry*, *180*, 461–464. https://doi.org/10.1192/bjp.180.5.461

Musick, M. A., Herzog, A. R., & House, J. S. (1999). Volunteering and mortality among older adults: Findings from a national sample. *Journals of Gerontology. Series B, Psychological Sciences and Social Sciences*, *54*(3), S173–80. https://doi.org/10.1093/geronb/54b.3.s173

Musick, M. A., & Wilson, J. (2003). Volunteering and depression: The role of psychological and social resources in different age groups. *Social Science & Medicine*, *56*(2), 259–269. https://doi.org/10.1016/s0277-9536(02)00025-4

Nelson, S. K., Layous, K., Cole, S. W., & Lyubomirsky, S. (2016). Do unto others or treat yourself? The effects of prosocial and self-focused behavior on psychological flourishing. *Emotion*, *16*(6), 850–861. https://doi.org/10.1037/emo0000178

Nierenberg, A. A., Keefe, B. R., Leslie, V. C., Alpert, J. E., Pava, J. A., Worthington, J. J., Rosenbaum, J. F., & Fava, M. (1999). Residual symptoms in depressed patients who respond acutely to fluoxetine. *Primary Care Companion to the Journal of Clinical Psychiatry*, *1*(4), 124.

Oman, D., Thoresen, C. E., & McMahon, K. (1999). Volunteerism and mortality among the community-dwelling elderly. *Journal of Health Psychology*, *4*(3), 301–316. https://doi.org/10.1177/135910539900400301

Otake, K., Shimai, S., Tanaka-Matsumi, J., Otsui, K., & Fredrickson, B. L. (2006). Happy people become happier through kindness: A counting kindnesses intervention. *Journal of Happiness Studies, 7*(3), 361–375. https://doi.org/10.1007/s10902-005-3650-z

Pelizza, L., & Ferrari, A. (2009). Anhedonia in schizophrenia and major depression: State or trait? *Annals of General Psychiatry, 8*(1), 22. https://doi.org/10.1186/1744-859X-8-22

Peters, J., & Büchel, C. (2010). Neural representations of subjective reward value. *Behavioural Brain Research, 213*(2), 135–141. https://doi.org/10.1016/j.bbr.2010.04.031

Peters, K. D., Constans, J. I., & Mathews, A. (2011). Experimental modification of attribution processes. *Journal of Abnormal Psychology, 120*(1), 168–173. https://doi.org/10.1037/a0021899

Pictet, A., Coughtrey, A. E., Mathews, A., & Holmes, E. A. (2011). Fishing for happiness: The effects of generating positive imagery on mood and behaviour. *Behaviour Research and Therapy, 49*(12), 885–891. https://doi.org/10.1016/j.brat.2011.10.003

Pictet, A., Jermann, F., & Ceschi, G. (2016). When less could be more: Investigating the effects of a brief internet-based imagery cognitive bias modification intervention in depression. *Behaviour Research and Therapy, 84,* 45–51. https://doi.org/10.1016/j.brat.2016.07.008

Pizzagalli, D. A., Holmes, A. J., Dillon, D. G., Goetz, E. L., Birk, J. L., Bogdan, R., Dougherty, D. D., Iosifescu, D. V., Rauch, S. L., & Fava, M. (2009). Reduced caudate and nucleus accumbens response to rewards in unmedicated individuals with major depressive disorder. *American Journal of Psychiatry, 166*(6), 702–710. https://doi.org/10.1176/appi.ajp.2008.08081201

Pizzagalli, D. A., Iosifescu, D., Hallett, L. A., Ratner, K. G., & Fava, M. (2008). Reduced hedonic capacity in major depressive disorder: Evidence from a probabilistic reward task. *Journal of Psychiatric Research, 43*(1), 76–87. https://doi.org/https://doi.org/10.1016/j.jpsychires.2008.03.001

Pizzagalli, D. A., Jahn, A. L., & O'Shea, J. P. (2005). Toward an objective characterization of an anhedonic phenotype: A signal-detection approach. *Biological Psychiatry, 57*(4), 319–327. https://doi.org/https://doi.org/10.1016/j.biopsych.2004.11.026

Pizzagalli, D. A., Smoski, M., Ang, Y. S., Whitton, A. E., Sanacora, G., Mathew, S. J., Nurnberger, J., Lisanby, S. H., Iosifescu, D. V., Murrough, J. W., Yang, H., Weiner, R. D., Calabrese, J. R., Goodman, W., Potter, W. Z., & Krystal, A. D. (2020). Selective kappa-opioid antagonism ameliorates anhedonic behavior: Evidence from the Fast-fail Trial in Mood and Anxiety Spectrum Disorders (FAST-MAS).

Neuropsychopharmacology, *45*(10), 1656–1663. https://doi.org/ 10.1038/s41386-020-0738-4

Price, J., Cole, V., & Goodwin, G. M. (2009). Emotional side-effects of selective serotonin reuptake inhibitors: Qualitative study. *British Journal of Psychiatry,* *195*(3), 211–217. https://doi.org/10.1192/bjp. bp.108.051110

Raposa, E. B., Laws, H. B., & Ansell, E. B. (2016). Prosocial behavior mitigates the negative effects of stress in everyday life. *Clinical Psychological Science,* *4*(4), 691–698. https://doi.org/10.1177/ 2167702615611073

Rizvi, S. J., Quilty, L. C., Sproule, B. A., Cyriac, A., Bagby, R. M., & Kennedy, S. H. (2015). Development and validation of the Dimensional Anhedonia Rating Scale (DARS) in a community sample and individuals with major depression. *Psychiatry Research,* *229*(1–2), 109–119. https://doi.org/10.1016/j.psychres.2015.07.062

Rowland, L., & Curry, O. S. (2019). A range of kindness activities boost happiness. *Journal of Social Psychology,* *159*(3), 340–343. https://doi. org/10.1080/00224545.2018.1469461

Rude, S. S., Wenzlaff, R. M., Gibbs, B., Vane, J., & Whitney, T. (2002). Negative processing biases predict subsequent depressive symptoms. *Cognition and Emotion,* *16*(3), 423–440. https://doi.org/10.1080/ 02699930143000554

Schacter, H. L., & Margolin, G. (2019). When it feels good to give: Depressive symptoms, daily prosocial behavior, and adolescent mood. *Emotion,* *19*(5), 923–927. https://doi.org/10.1037/emo0000494

Shane, M. S., & Peterson, J. B. (2007). An evaluation of early and late stage attentional processing of positive and negative information in dysphoria. *Cognition and Emotion,* *21*(4), 789–815. https://doi.org/ 10.1080/02699930600843197

Shankman, S. A., & Klein, D. N. (2003). The relation between depression and anxiety: An evaluation of the tripartite, approach-withdrawal and valence-arousal models. *Clinical Psychology Review,* *23*(4), 605–637. https://doi.org/https://doi.org/10.1016/S0272-7358(03)00038-2

Shonin, E., Van Gordon, W., Compare, A., Zangeneh, M., & Griffiths, M. D. (2015). Buddhist-derived loving-kindness and compassion meditation for the treatment of psychopathology: A systematic review. *Mindfulness,* *6*(5), 1161–1180. https://doi.org/10.1007/s12671-014-0368-1

Smith, N. K., Larsen, J. T., Chartrand, T. L., Cacioppo, J. T., Katafiasz, H. A., & Moran, K. E. (2006). Being bad isn't always good: Affective context moderates the attention bias toward negative information. *Journal of Personality and Social Psychology, 90*(2), 210–220). https://doi.org/10.1037/0022-3514.90.2.210

Snaith, R. P., Hamilton, M., Morley, S., Humayan, A., Hargreaves, D., & Trigwell, P. (1995). A scale for the assessment of hedonic tone. The Snaith-Hamilton Pleasure Scale. *British Journal of Psychiatry, 167*(1), 99–103. https://doi.org/10.1192/bjp.167.1.99

Snippe, E., Jeronimus, B. F., Aan Het Rot, M., Bos, E. H., de Jonge, P., & Wichers, M. (2018). The reciprocity of prosocial behavior and positive affect in daily life. *Journal of Personality, 86*(2), 139–146. https://doi.org/10.1111/jopy.12299

Speer, M. E., Bhanji, J. P., & Delgado, M. R. (2014). Savoring the past: Positive memories evoke value representations in the striatum. *Neuron, 84*(4), 847–856. https://doi.org/10.1016/j.neuron.2014.09.028

Spijker, J., De Graaf, R., Ten Have, M., Nolen, W. A., & Speckens, A. (2010). Predictors of suicidality in depressive spectrum disorders in the general population: Results of the Netherlands Mental Health Survey and Incidence Study. *Social Psychiatry and Psychiatric Epidemiology, 45*(5), 513–521. https://doi.org/10.1007/s00127-009-0093-6

Srivastava, S., Sharma, H. O., & Mandal, M. K. (2003). Mood induction with facial expressions of emotion in patients with generalized anxiety disorder. *Depression and Anxiety, 18*(3), 144–148. https://doi.org/10.1002/da.10128

Stöber, J. (2000). Prospective cognitions in anxiety and depression: Replication and methodological extension. *Cognition and Emotion, 14*(5), 725–729. https://doi.org/10.1080/02699930050117693

Stoy, M., Schlagenhauf, F., Sterzer, P., Bermpohl, F., Hägele, C., Suchotzki, K., Schmack, K., Wrase, J., Ricken, R., Knutson, B., Adli, M., Bauer, M., Heinz, A., & Ströhle, A. (2012). Hyporeactivity of ventral striatum towards incentive stimuli in unmedicated depressed patients normalizes after treatment with escitalopram. *Journal of Psychopharmacology, 26*(5), 677–688. https://doi.org/10.1177/0269881111416686

Thoits, P. A., & Hewitt, L. N. (2001). Volunteer work and well-being. *Journal of Health and Social Behavior, 42*(2), 115–131.

Thomas, R. K., Baker, G., Lind, J., & Dursun, S. (2018). Rapid effectiveness of intravenous ketamine for ultraresistant depression in a clinical setting and evidence for baseline anhedonia and bipolarity as clinical predictors of effectiveness. *Journal of Psychopharmacology, 32*(10), 1110–1117. https://doi.org/10.1177/0269881118793104

Thomsen, K. R., Whybrow, P. C., & Kringelbach, M. L. (2015). Reconceptualizing anhedonia: Novel perspectives on balancing the pleasure networks in the human brain. *Frontiers in Behavioral Neuroscience, 9*, 49. https://doi.org/10.3389/fnbeh.2015.00049

Treadway, M. T., Bossaller, N. A., Shelton, R. C., & Zald, D. H. (2012). Effort-based decision-making in major depressive disorder: A translational model of motivational anhedonia. *Journal of Abnormal Psychology, 121*(3), 553–558. https://doi.org/10.1037/a0028813

Trivers, R. L. (1971). The evolution of reciprocal altruism. *Quarterly Review of Biology, 46*(1), 35–57. https://doi.org/10.1086/406755

Tsvetkova, M., & Macy, M. W. (2014). The social contagion of generosity. *PloS One, 9*(2), e87275. https://doi.org/10.1371/journal.pone.0087275

Tugade, M. M., & Fredrickson, B. L. (2004). Resilient individuals use positive emotions to bounce back from negative emotional experiences. *Journal of Personality and Social Psychology, 86*(2), 320–333. https://doi.org/10.1037/0022-3514.86.2.320

Ubl, B., Kuehner, C., Kirsch, P., Ruttorf, M., Diener, C., & Flor, H. (2015). Altered neural reward and loss processing and prediction error signalling in depression. *Social Cognitive and Affective Neuroscience, 10*(8), 1102–1112. https://doi.org/10.1093/scan/nsu158

Van Overwalle, F., Mervielde, I., & De Schuyter, J. (1995). Structural modelling of the relationships between attributional dimensions, emotions, and performance of college freshmen. *Cognition and Emotion, 9*(1), 59–85. https://doi.org/10.1080/02699939508408965

Vinckier, F., Gourion, D., & Mouchabac, S. (2017). Anhedonia predicts poor psychosocial functioning: Results from a large cohort of patients treated for major depressive disorder by general practitioners. *European Psychiatry, 44*, 1–8. https://doi.org/10.1016/j.eurpsy.2017.02.485

Vrieze, E., Pizzagalli, D. A., Demyttenaere, K., Hompes, T., Sienaert, P., de Boer, P., Schmidt, M., & Claes, S. (2013). Reduced reward learning predicts outcome in major depressive disorder. *Biological Psychiatry, 73*(7), 639–645. https://doi.org/https://doi.org/10.1016/j.biopsych.2012.10.014

Wacker, J., Dillon, D. G., & Pizzagalli, D. A. (2009). The role of the nucleus accumbens and rostral anterior cingulate cortex in anhedonia: Integration of resting EEG, fMRI, and volumetric techniques. *NeuroImage, 46*(1), 327–337. https://doi.org/10.1016/j.neuroimage.2009.01.058

Wadlinger, H. A., & Isaacowitz, D. M. (2008). Looking happy: The experimental manipulation of a positive visual attention bias. *Emotion, 8*(1), 121–126. https://doi.org/10.1037/1528-3542.8.1.121

Wadlinger, H. A., & Isaacowitz, D. M. (2011). Fixing our focus: Training attention to regulate emotion. *Personality and Social Psychology Review, 15*(1), 75–102. https://doi.org/10.1177/1088868310365565

Watson, D., Clark, L. A., & Tellegen, A. (1988). Development and validation of brief measures of positive and negative affect: The PANAS scales. *Journal of Personality and Social Psychology, 54*(6), 1063–1070. https://doi.org/10.1037/0022-3514.54.6.1063

Werner-Seidler, A., & Moulds, M. L. (2011). Autobiographical memory characteristics in depression vulnerability: Formerly depressed individuals recall less vivid positive memories. *Cognition and Emotion, 25*(6), 1087–1103. https://doi.org/10.1080/02699931.2010.531007

Whitton, A. E., Treadway, M. T., & Pizzagalli, D. A. (2015). Reward processing dysfunction in major depression, bipolar disorder and schizophrenia. *Current Opinion in Psychiatry, 28*(1), 7–12. https://journals.lww.com/co-psychiatry/Fulltext/2015/01000/Reward_processing_dysfunction_in_major_depression,.3.aspx

Wichers, M., Peeters, F., Geschwind, N., Jacobs, N., Simons, C. J. P., Derom, C., Thiery, E., Delespaul, P. H., & van Os, J. (2010). Unveiling patterns of affective responses in daily life may improve outcome prediction in depression: A momentary assessment study. *Journal of Affective Disorders, 124*(1–2), 191–195. https://doi.org/10.1016/j.jad.2009.11.010

Williams, J. M. G., Barnhofer, T., Crane, C., Herman, D., Raes, F., Watkins, E., & Dalgleish, T. (2007). Autobiographical memory specificity and emotional disorder. *Psychological Bulletin, 133*(1), 122–148. https://doi.org/10.1037/0033-2909.133.1.122

Winer, E. S., Nadorff, M. R., Ellis, T. E., Allen, J. G., Herrera, S., & Salem, T. (2014). Anhedonia predicts suicidal ideation in a large psychiatric inpatient sample. *Psychiatry Research, 218*(1–2), 124–128. https://doi.org/10.1016/j.psychres.2014.04.016

Wood, A. M., Froh, J. J., & Geraghty, A. W. A. (2010). Gratitude and well-being: A review and theoretical integration. *Clinical Psychology Review, 30*(7), 890–905. https://doi.org/10.1016/j.cpr.2010.03.005

Wood, A. M., Joseph, S., & Maltby, J. (2008a). Gratitude uniquely predicts satisfaction with life: Incremental validity above the domains and facets of the five factor model. *Personality and Individual Differences, 45*(1), 49–54. https://doi.org/https://doi.org/10.1016/j.paid.2008.02.019

Wood, A. M., Maltby, J., Gillett, R., Linley, P. A., & Joseph, S. (2008b). The role of gratitude in the development of social support, stress, and depression: Two longitudinal studies. *Journal of Research in*

Personality, 42(4), 854–871. https://doi.org/https://doi.org/10.1016/j.jrp.2007.11.003

Wood, A. M., Maltby, J., Stewart, N., & Joseph, S. (2008c). Conceptualizing gratitude and appreciation as a unitary personality trait. *Personality and Individual Differences, 44*(3), 621–632. https://doi.org/https://doi.org/10.1016/j.paid.2007.09.028

Yang, X., Huang, J., Zhu, C., Wang, Y., Cheung, E. F. C., Chan, R. C. K., & Xie, G. (2014). Motivational deficits in effort-based decision making in individuals with subsyndromal depression, first-episode and remitted depression patients. *Psychiatry Research, 220*(3), 874–882. https://doi.org/10.1016/j.psychres.2014.08.056

Yang, Z. Y., Xie, D. J., Zou, Y. M., Wang, Y., Li, Y., Shi, H. S., Zhang, R. T., Li, W. X., Cheung, E. F. C., Kring, A. M., & Chan, R. C. K. (2018). Prospection deficits in schizophrenia: Evidence from clinical and subclinical samples. *Journal of Abnormal Psychology, 127*(7), 710–721. https://doi.org/10.1037/abn0000382

Zak, P. J., Stanton, A. A., & Ahmadi, S. (2007). Oxytocin increases generosity in humans. *PloS One, 2*(11), e1128. https://doi.org/10.1371/journal.pone.0001128

Zeng, X., Chiu, C. P. K., Wang, R., Oei, T. P. S., & Leung, F. Y. K. (2015). The effect of loving-kindness meditation on positive emotions: A meta-analytic review. *Frontiers in Psychology, 6*, 1693. https://www.frontiersin.org/article/10.3389/fpsyg.2015.01693

Zeng, X., Liao, R., Zhang, R., Oei, T. P. S., Yao, Z., Leung, F. Y. K., & Liu, X. (2017). Development of the Appreciative Joy Scale. *Mindfulness, 8*(2), 286–299. https://doi.org/10.1007/s12671-016-0599-4

Zeng, X., Wang, R., Oei, T. P. S., & Leung, F. Y. K. (2019). Heart of joy: A randomized controlled trial evaluating the effect of an appreciative joy meditation training on subjective well-being and attitudes. *Mindfulness, 10*(3), 506–515. https://doi.org/10.1007/s12671-018-0992-2

Zielinski, M. J., Veilleux, J. C., Winer, E. S., & Nadorff, M. R. (2017). A short-term longitudinal examination of the relations between depression, anhedonia, and self-injurious thoughts and behaviors in adults with a history of self-injury. *Comprehensive Psychiatry, 73*, 187–195. https://doi.org/10.1016/j.comppsych.2016.11.013

Michelle G. Craske, PhD, is Professor of Psychology, Psychiatry and Biobehavioral Sciences, Miller Endowed Term Chair, Director of the Anxiety and Depression Research Center, and Associate Director of the Staglin Family Music Center for Behavioral and Brain Health, at the University of California, Los Angeles. She is also co-director of the UCLA Depression Grand Challenge. She has researched and published extensively in the area of fear, anxiety, and depression and is on the Web of Science Most Highly Cited Researcher List. She has been the recipient of extramural funding for research projects pertaining to risk factors for anxiety and depression among children and adolescents, neural mediators of emotion regulation and behavioral treatments for anxiety disorders, fear extinction translational models for optimizing exposure therapy, novel behavioral therapies targeting reward sensitivity and anhedonia, and scalable treatment models for underserved populations. She has received multiple awards of distinction. At UCLA, she received the Society of Postdoctoral Scholars at UCLA Mentorship Award and Career Development Award. Nationally, she received the American Psychological Association Society for a Science of Clinical Psychology Distinguished Scientist Award, the Outstanding Researcher Award from the Association for Behavioral and Cognitive Therapy, and the Aaron T. Beck Award from the Academy of Cognitive Therapy. Internationally, she was awarded the International Francqui Professorship from Belgium, and the Eleonore Trefftz Guest Professorship Award from the Technical University of Dresden, Germany. She received an honorary doctorate from Maastricht University, Netherlands, and is an honorary fellow of the Department of Psychiatry, Oxford University, and an honorary fellow of the Dutch-Flemish Postgraduate School for Research and Education. Further, she has been president of the APA Society for a Science of Clinical Psychology and the Association for Behavioral and Cognitive Therapy. She is Editor-in-Chief for *Behaviour Research* *and Therapy*. Dr. Craske received her BA Hons from the University of Tasmania and her PhD from the University of British Columbia.

Halina J. Dour, PhD, is the owner of the Center for Genuine Growth, a multi-state telepsychology practice. Dr. Dour spent most of her post-doctoral career within Veterans Affairs (VA) healthcare systems. She served as the Eating Disorder Team Coordinator and as a member of the PTSD Clinical Team within the Orlando VA Healthcare System. Prior to this, she spent nearly two years as a clinical psychologist in the Mental Health Clinic and Intensive Outpatient Program at the VA Puget Sound, Seattle Division. Dr. Dour has been trained in numerous evidence-based treatments and worked in a variety of settings. This, coupled with a passion for creating interventions, therapy materials, and program-ming, has led Dr. Dour to gain a specific expertise in treatment and program development. She has served, and continues to serve, as a con-sultant on multiple treatment development projects. Dr. Dour received her bachelor's degree *cum laude* in psychology from Wellesley College and her PhD in Clinical Psychology from the University of California, Los Angeles, where she studied under the mentorship of Dr. Michelle Craske. During her doctoral training, she earned numerous awards and fellowships, including the National Science Foundation Fellowship, the University Distinguished Fellowship, the Ursula-Mandel Stipend Award, the Philip & Aida Siff Award, the UCLA Affiliates Award, the Senior Clinical Scientist Award, the Outstanding SSCP Student Clinician Award, and the APA Div12 Distinguished Student Practice in Clinical Psychology Award. Dr. Dour completed her predoctoral intern-ship at the VA Sepulveda Ambulatory Care Center and her postdoctoral fellowship at the VA Puget Sound, Seattle Division.

Michael Treanor, PhD, is an Assistant Project Scientist with the UCLA Anxiety and Depression Research Center. His research focuses on improving exposure therapy for posttraumatic stress disorder and anxiety-related disorders, and he has extensive experience in numerous evidence-based treatments for PTSD, anxiety disorders, and mood disorders, including mindfulness practices. Along with Dr. Dour and Dr. Craske, he developed the original content of Positive Affect Treatment. Dr. Treanor is a principal investigator and clinical supervisor for ongoing psychological treatment trials at the UCLA Anxiety and Depression Research Center and provides therapist training in evidence-based therapies, including Positive Affect Treatment, for psychiatry and psychology fellows. Dr. Treanor completed an APA-approved internship at the National Center for PTSD, Behavioral Science Division at the Boston VA, and a National Institute of Mental Health T32 postdoctoral fellowship at UCLA.

Alicia E. Meuret, PhD, is a Professor at the Department of Psychology at Southern Methodist University (SMU), the Director of the SMU Anxiety and Depression Research Center, and a licensed clinical psychologist. She completed her doctoral studies at Stanford University Department of Psychiatry and Behavioral Sciences and her postdoctoral studies at the Affective Neuroscience Laboratory at Harvard University and the Center for Anxiety and Related Disorders at Boston University. Her research program focuses on novel treatment approaches for anxiety and mood disorders, biomarkers in anxiety disorders and chronic disease (asthma), fear extinction mechanisms of exposure therapy, and mediators and moderators in individuals with affective dysregulations, including non-suicidal self-injury. Dr. Meuret is the founder of Capnometry-Assisted Respiratory Training (CART). Dr. Meuret has published over 100 scientific publications and authored over 200 conference presentations. Her work has received ongoing funding from the National Institutes of Health and other funding agencies. She has received multiple honors, including from the Anxiety and Depression Association of America, the Psychiatric Research Society, and the American Psychosomatic Society. She is a Beck Institute Fellow and a Rotunda Outstanding Professor. Dr. Meuret is a member of the Scientific Advisory Board of the Anxiety and Depression Association of America, was past president of the International Society of the Advancement of Respiratory Psychophysiology, and is a fellow of the Association of Cognitive and Behavioral Therapies. As a technical expert, she assisted the Agency for Healthcare Research and Quality Effective Health Care Program and was on the Scientific Advisory Board of the Centre for Excellence at the University of Leuven, Belgium. Dr. Meuret serves on several editorial boards and was an Associate Editor for Behavior Therapy. Dr. Meuret has more than 20 years of clinical experience treating patients with emotional disorders.